I Do -- Again

A 30-day devotional filled with
practical advice, proactive intervention,
and positive encouragement for
couples in their second or subsequent marriage.

by Patrick and Donna Schlachter

ISBN: 978-1-943688-22-7

Published by: PLS Bookworks, Denver, Colorado

PLS

Where Publishing Dreams Become Reality

Dedication

First and foremost to the glory of God; His Risen Son, Jesus Christ, our personal Lord and Savior; and to the Holy Spirit, who leads and counsels us.

To the memory of J.W. and Doris Setliff, the best example of marriage and togetherness this side of heaven, and

To our daughters, Lyndsey and Elizabeth (Beth) -- in God, in order.

Other Books by Patrick and Donna Schlachter

Non-fiction

Quiet Moments Alone with God, Baker Publishing

100 Answers to 100 Questions about Loving Your Husband, Strang Communications

Broken Dreams, Mended Heart: 21 days to the spiritual healing you've always wanted, PLS Bookworks

Broken Dreams, Mended Marriage: 21 days to the marriage you've always wanted, PLS Bookworks

Nuggets of Writing Gold, with Leeann Betts, PLS Bookworks

Fiction

Second Chances and Second Cups, PLS Bookworks

Writing as Leeann Betts

By the Numbers series: *No Accounting for Murder; There Was a Crooked Man; Unbalanced; Five and Twenty Blackbirds*, all from PLS Bookworks

Counting the Days: a 30-day devotional for accountants, bookkeepers, and financial folk, PLS Bookworks

All books available at Amazon.com

Introduction

There is an old joke about Christopher Columbus: he didn't know where he was going, he didn't know where he was when he got there, and he did it all on borrowed money.

In many ways, remarriage can seem a lot like old Chris's journey. You don't know where you are going with this new marriage, you may not recognize it when you get there, and you are doing it based on perceptions and memories borrowed from a previous marriage journey.

Remarriage takes many forms, and can include various and sundry step-children, step-grandchildren, in-laws, old and new families trying to meld together into one happy family. And in the midst of all this melding, life comes along. Jobs, careers, finances, elder issues – all add more stressors to an equation that seems unbalanced to begin with.

And you're right, it is unbalanced. Remarriage is seldom fair, seldom equal, seldom what you were expecting. Whether you are just contemplating getting remarried, have been married for a few years, or are celebrating another major milestone anniversary for the second time, this devotional book will help you on the journey.

This is not another marriage-counseling book, although there are some sound marriage principles included. This is not a child-raising book, although you will probably glean some wisdom to apply to your family situation. This is not a financial counseling book, but you will see some suggestions as to how to relieve financial pressures.

This is a day-to-day living book, based on scriptural principles, grounded in experience, and pointing you to God for every aspect of your remarriage. God's goal for your marriage is to glorify Himself, to demonstrate His love for His kids, to raise up a new generation of followers, and to complete you and your spouse in

Him.

Use this book as a devotional to direct your day, as a couple Bible Study to teach new principles, as a quick-fix tool for specific areas of your marriage where you struggle. However you use it, ask God to show you what He wants you to learn, and to draw you closer together as a couple.

We pray God's blessings on you as you invest in your marriage, one scripture verse at a time, one precept at a time, one day at a time.

Patrick and Donna Schlachter

His Family, Her Family, Our Family

Who am I, O Lord God, and what is my family
that you have given me all this?
I Chronicles 17:16 TLB

Peace in the Family

Isn't it obvious that your God is present with you; that He has given you
peaceful relations with everyone around?
(1 Chronicles 22:18 The Message)

There are many blended families in America today, but our current family came when Donna was forty years old. She became a mother by marrying a father who was also a grandfather. Joining two separate entities together is a challenge at the best of times, without bringing rivalries and personalities into the equation.

Donna talked to 'her' daughters on the telephone several times. She had seen pictures of the grandkids. She heard some stories from Patrick about his memories of the girls' growing up years. But nothing could have prepared her for the sight of two beautiful women draped over her husband-to-be. And when we say beautiful, we mean just that. The older one, pregnant with her third child, glowed. The younger one, getting ready to start her senior year of high school, had that innocent, girl-next-door beauty that all the boys fall for. And here they were, hanging all over Patrick! Wherever we went, at least one of them clung to his arm or held his hand. And Donna found it very disconcerting to see one of them suddenly wrap her arms around his neck and plant a big kiss on his cheek.

Was Donna jealous? At first she was. She found herself sidling up to them, wriggling her way into their midst to stand next to Patrick, staking out her territory, as it were. Or she watched from a distance, envious of their youth, their beauty, the relationship they had with their dad.

Then she realized how foolish she was acting. She was not a jealous, insecure teenager; she was a mature woman. There was no competition from these young women, except for his time. Donna had the rest of her life to spend with him, while they had only a few days before they headed home, over 600 miles away. Once she saw there was room in his heart for three beautiful women, she relaxed. The transition has not been easy, but it is getting easier.

Family is more than just you as a couple. And it is more than one parent and their children. It is all of you, together.

Lord, remind me that I am part of a bigger family, Your family. And that in your family, I'm never an outsider. Amen

Take-Away for Today

Send a card to your step-kids telling them how glad you are to be in their family. If you don't have step-kids, send a card to your in-laws.

Sweet Melody

God has so composed the body, giving the greater honor to the
inferior part,
that there may be no discord in the body, but that the members
may have the same care for one another.
(1 Corinthians 12:24-25 ASV)

Consider for a moment the process of composing a piece of
music. Every composer begins with the same elements: the notes.
Then each composer decides what kind of music he is going to write:
country, jazz, classical, rock. Then he sets about to combine the
elements of music into a tune that is pleasing to the ear. He chooses
notes and sets them to a beat, placing each one carefully within its
measure, then strings the measures together to create a bar, and then
finally a melody.

Combining a family can be much like writing a piece of
music. Begin by deciding what kind of a family you would like to
have: laid back, constantly busy, mother stays at home, kids visit on
weekends.

Start with the components of your family, just as a composer
starts with the basic elements of music, the notes. Decide what kind
of structure works best for your lifestyle, just as the composer
decides what he wants his music to do, what audience he wants to
reach.

Consider the individuals who make up your new combined
family. It is important to remember they are just that – individuals.
No matter how hard you try, you are not going to make everyone
happy. Your goal is not individual happiness, but family happiness.
And that can sometimes mean that not all the individuals are ecstatic
about a decision.

When you keep your remarriage as the focus of the family,
you will find most other things falling into place. The relationship

between God, husband, and wife is the reason for this marriage, and you must keep that as the primary goal.

God designed marriage to edify and encourage the husband and the wife, to cause them to stretch beyond what they could do on their own, and to show His love to others around them. Begin to edify and encourage each other by reminding yourselves that your spouse is a perfect gift from God. Remind each other that a three-stranded cord is stronger than a single thread. And, encourage each other with the reminder that children are a blessing from God.

An important thing to remember about music also applies to families – not all the notes sound the same. Translated to the family situation, what works with one child will not work with all of the children. This applies to demonstrations of affection, need for personal time, abilities, discipline, and relationship building. Just as a composer does not pick one note and try to make a song out of it, you cannot expect your children to all fit into the same mold.

Trying to force all the children to be the same will simply tear you apart. Instead of laying down hard and fast rules, consider the entire household, the activities going on, the ages and maturity of the children, and your goals for your family.

For example, suppose both parents work all day and just want to come home to a clean, quiet house. In that case, letting the kids congregate at your house after school will not be conducive to your goal. On the other hand, if one parent is at home during the day and you love to know what your kids are up to, this would work well for you.

When you have a houseful of toddlers and one lone teenager who visits a couple of weekends a month, setting up a room for the teenager where he can be by himself, instead of being constantly surrounded by kids, will allow the older child private time, while at the same time allowing him to choose when to be part of the family activities.

Encourage your kids to get active in after-school or weekend activities, as opposed to those held in the evenings, if your goal is to have family dinner every evening.

If you have children who stay over with another parent several times a month, do not plan any family activities while they are gone. Instead, schedule date night or spend time individually with one of the other kids.

With children who visit your home several times a month, think about ways to include them in your regular activities. For example, you can check with the Children's Church leader at your church, explain the situation, and see if you can get handouts for the weeks your child will be away.

Encourage the children who live with you to schedule their activities with the visiting child's schedule in mind, but do not insist their plans must revolve around the visiting sibling all the time. If you do, the children who live with you may become resentful of the intrusion into their schedule. Remember, the point of the sibling visits is also to spend time with their biological parent, so schedule in some time for that, too.

When you take a good look at your family, you will find there are many ways to combine the individuals. God's desire is that your remarriage succeed, and that can be accomplished by keeping the marriage first, by being flexible in how you combine the different elements of the marriage, and by desiring to show love and concern to each member.

God, only You can bring all these different parts together and make it into a beautiful cohesive unit. I place my family into Your hands. Amen.

Take-Away for Today

Create an Activity Center for your family. Start with a large wall calendar, then assign different colors for each person, and a separate color for those things the family will do together. Write in all the activities and appointments currently scheduled before you make decisions about adding any. Take a look at the calendar – is there anybody who has few activities scheduled? Do you have at least one family activity per week, even if it is only dinner together? Don't forget your couple date night, as well as one-on-one time with each child. Be sure everyone in the family understands that they have to check the schedule before committing to any other activities. Set aside one evening a month to sit down as a family and discuss the schedule.

Generational Blessings

Sons and daughters, come and listen and let me teach you
the importance of trusting and fearing the Lord.
(Psalm 34:11 TLB)

Many times, remarrieds find themselves with a whole new set of family members, including in-laws, children, and grandchildren. It can be hard enough to develop a relationship with children who live under your roof or who at least come to visit on a regular basis. When it comes to grandchildren, however, it can be even harder to develop a relationship.

Not every transition into a remarried family goes smoothly. What do you do when there is resistance? Depending on circumstances, ages, and personalities involved, you can be faced with what seems like an uphill battle. Still, there are some important things to remember.

First of all, God put you together as a couple for His plan, not for yours. We all come into a remarriage with some unrealistic expectations, no matter why your previous marriage ended.

Unrealistic expectations always set you up for failure. People rarely do what you want them to do just because you want them to do it. And grandchildren are people. If you can remember that they are individuals and not an extension of your children, you will be able to treat them that way.

Second, remind yourselves that you married your spouse, not their family. While it is normal to want a good relationship with the children and grandchildren, you cannot determine the success or failure of your marriage based on that relationship.

Third, God is the One in control, not you. You cannot force the grandchildren to like you. You cannot change to become the grandparent they want you to be. Only God can change the hearts of everyone involved.

Studies have shown there are three ways remarrieds try to integrate themselves into their stepfamily's lives: aloofness, smothering, and something in between.

To no one's surprise, the something in between is the most successful. Letting them know you care about them, you want what's best for them, and you are there when they need you is the way to let the step-family, particularly children and grandchildren, get to know you.

When you express an interest in what they do without judging them, you show them that you want to spend time with them on common ground. When you let them see some of the things that you are interested in, you show them that you are willing to teach without preaching. When you talk to them about their dreams and feelings, you validate their concerns.

One way to show that you really want to be a family is to create some new traditions with the grandkids. Major holidays are a good time to do this, since kids already expect traditions.

These new traditions can be a combination of old and new, or they can be an old one from your childhood that is new to them.

Include an explanation of the tradition, even if that means doing some research. Sometimes traditions are handed down in families without any understanding of their origin. In order to make them real and important to your new family, understand why you do it. 'Because we've done that in my family for generations' is not the way to solidify your new family.

Make sure that the traditions you choose have happy memories associated with them. When you share those memories, especially if they include people your grandkids already know, you create a sense of family, of continuity, and of belonging. One of the biggest problems that stepchildren face is the sense of not belonging to any one family. You can show your stepchildren and step-grandchildren that they belong in your family now by including them in those traditions.

God has given you children and grandchildren as a blessing to you and to them. They are on loan from Him, and your goal is to show His love to them. Create some wonderful memories with these blessings, and they will bless you in return.

Father, thank You for the blessing of children and grandchildren. Show me how to love them like You love them. Amen.

Take-Away for Today

Go through your photo albums, and create a new album for each of your grandchildren, including pictures of your parents and grandparents, siblings, cousins, etc. as well as from your spouse's side of the family. Include some pictures of you and your spouse, as well as some of your children and grandchildren from this marriage. Give the album as a "just because" gift, explaining that you want your families to be one family now.

As Days Go By

Honor your father and mother.
Then you will live a long, full life.
(Exodus 20:12 NLT)

God tells us to honor our parents. This honor is given to thank them for raising us, for providing for us, and for giving us godly role models to emulate. We are to honor them even if they made a mess of things. We are to learn from their mistakes and not make the same ones with our own kids. Showing godly love to our parents is the highest form of honor.

Sometimes honoring our parents will mean going against what they taught us. This is true if they are not believers in Christ. The best way we can honor our parents is to live the life God planned for us to live, honoring Him as our Heavenly Father.

It is a fact that people are living longer. Back in the early 1900's a person could expect to live to be around 60. Today, the expected life span in the United States is in the '80s.

That's really good news for those who look forward to those years, but it also means that, statistically speaking, there is a very good chance you will have at least one grandparent or parent who will be living out their last years in your home.

Many times this happens just when you think you can sit back and relax. The kids are grown and out of the home, you are settled in your career and looking forward to taking it easy.

Being a remarried means you have already dealt with the awkward situation of combining two families into a cohesive unit. And this was done with reasonably healthy individuals. But bringing an elderly parent or grandparent into the home is not usually done under such ideal circumstances.

There are many reasons to consider having an elder move into your home. Sometimes the death of their spouse upsets them to the point where they cannot cope. This is often the case when the more dominant elder passes away first, leaving the other completely unprepared for living on their own.

Another reason is poor health. Many times an elder will break a bone, such as a hip, which incapacitates them so they cannot live by themselves. Mental stability can often deteriorate as parents age, causing a loss of memory and cognitive skills. Inability to drive can strand an elder in their home. Chronic illness such as diabetes or arthritis can debilitate to the point of needing assistance.

So here you are, not really prepared for the situation you are faced with – an elder moving into your home. What can you expect?

In many ways, accepting that your elders are not the immortals you once thought them to be can be a lot like grief. These elders were integral to your growing up years, and now the roles are reversed. The child has become the parent, and the parent the child. Your perception of your elders has died, to be replaced with a new perception. And so in many ways you will grieve that loss.

Initially you can expect denial. There is no way this vigorous man who taught you to fish or play baseball or ride your bike isn't able to look after himself.

Then you will experience anger. How dare your mother not just get up and do what she needs to do to make her meals or even take a bath?

The next step will be guilt. You should have seen it coming, you should have been able to know that Grandmother was so bereft when Grandfather died that she wouldn't be able to cope. How could you have not seen that?

Finally, acceptance will come when you understand this isn't all about you. This isn't all about them. This is about God's plan for your life and for theirs. This is about an opportunity for you to show His love in a difficult situation. Coming to the realization that God knew about this from the beginning of time will help you put it in the proper perspective.

Admitting you cannot do it on your own will cause you to enlist the help of others, including God. Other family members, government services, friends in a similar situation – all can help you decide the best path to choose.

Sometimes we might think that having the elder move in with you is the best solution, because it seems to be the best for us. However, it might not be the best for the elder. Consider alternatives, such as an assisted living situation. Maybe there is a single person in your church who would like to exchange a room and board situation for acting as a companion to your elder.

Check with other family members to see if it would be feasible to share the burden by having the elder stay several months at a time with each sibling. This works especially well if you live in different climate zones so the elder can spend the winter in the sun and summer in the mountains, for example.

The decision to take an elder into your home must be a joint decision with your spouse. It's easy to bring your own mother or grandfather into your home, but how would you feel if your spouse made that decision about their elder relative without your agreement?

God in his wisdom has chosen you to be the caregivers to His elderly. He has given them long years and much wisdom and knowledge. When you encourage them to share that wisdom and knowledge with your children and with you, you forge strong relationships and create happy family memories.

Remember, some day you will be an elder, and you will hope for someone to care for you as well as you are caring for your elder now. Set the example for your children and grandchildren on how to honor their father and their mother.

Heavenly Father, thank You for entrusting me with the care of those who once cared for me. You tell me to cast my cares upon You, and so I give them over to You. Amen.

Take-Away for Today

Talk with your spouse about the possibilities of being required to bring an elder into your home. Discuss options. Make a list of resources you could call upon to make the transition and experience easier. Talk to your elders and ask them what they would should the need to move from their home or they need extra help. Talk to your siblings to see what they would like to do when the time arises. Talk to your children about your wishes for when the time comes that you are an elder in need of assistance.

Write all of this down so there is no confusion in the future, and make sure your last will and testament is in order, and where your children can find it.

His Life, Her Life, Our Life

Some trust in chariots, others in horses,
but you trust the LORD your God.
(Psalm 20:7 NCV)

Safe and Secure

We can go to God with bold confidence through faith in Christ.
(Ephesians 3:12 God's Word)

When Donna first suspected she was pregnant, she was afraid to tell Patrick, not knowing how he would take the news. After all, we hadn't exactly planned this pregnancy. In fact, when we'd discussed children before you got married, Donna told Patrick that she'd had her tubes tied three years before, thinking she was too old to start having babies. His response was, "We'll trust God. If He wants us to have children, He'll arrange it."

Donna need not have feared. When she mentioned, somewhat casually, that she was feeling nauseous, Patrick's whole face lit up, he smiled from ear to ear, and said, "Maybe you're not feeling good because you're pregnant."

And yet she was afraid to tell her husband about this miracle. Would he be jealous of a baby? Did he really want another child? He already had grown daughters from a previous marriage. Our baby would be younger than our grandchildren. What about his daughters? Would they feel threatened by another child?

As we talked, excitedly, about the possibility that Donna was pregnant, she knew without a doubt that God had worked a great miracle. She saw He had answered prayers, just as He has answered the prayers of many barren women before. We were reminded of Hannah and of Sarah, who had both waited many years for a child. Donna shared a story with Patrick about an incident that had happened the year before you were married.

Donna has a very dear friend who drew her into their family when Donna's first marriage ended. This friend had a wonderful husband and two darling children, and Donna spent a lot of time at her home. One day after dinner, she stood at the kitchen window, watching them playing together as a family. Her eyes filled with tears, and she prayed, "God, I want to have what she has." She did not want her friend's husband and kids; rather, she wanted a husband and children of her own. And then, a year later, God brought us together.

Although we were never blessed to hold our baby in this life, God has found other ways to fulfill the desires of your hearts. When we married, Donna became an instant mother and grandmother. God put the desire for a husband and children in her heart. He has gifted her with two beautiful daughters and ten delightful grandchildren.

Whatever else God has planned for us, we will be there. Just as He is there for you.

Lord, thank You for my children, my grandchildren, and the promises in You of much, much more. Amen.

Take-Away for Today
Go through your old photographs of your children and grandchildren, and create a collage for each of them.

Misunderstandings

Make your ear attentive to wisdom, incline your heart to
understanding.
(Proverbs 2:2 NAS)

Recently we were picking up food from a supermarket and
delivering it to a local mission. We were packing the boxes of food
in the midst of vendors bringing in their products and the area was
quite busy. Space was at a premium and we were under a time
constraint to be somewhere else very soon.

We wheeled the food through a maze of boxes and loaded
our van. While Donna was taking the carts back into the store,
Patrick said, "I'll move the van so I'm not in the way of these other
vendors. I'll just park over there." He pointed to an area of the
parking lot that was empty.

Donna said, "Fine, I'll come out through here." When she
came out, the van was driving down the street, with Patrick behind
the wheel. She started to run after it, and then stopped. She was
fuming! Her first thoughts were: is he trying to make me look
stupid? Why would he say he'd park here and then drive around to
the front of the store?

She punched his cell number on her phone. When he
answered, she was not pleasant.

"Where are you going? Why did not you wait for me like you
said you would?" she demanded.

"I thought you said you were going through the store," he
said.

"No, I said wait here for me. Where are you?"

"I'm looking at the front of the store."

Donna was not happy when she climbed into the van. Later,

when she managed to calm down enough to talk about it, she realized Patrick had simply misheard her.

This simple misunderstanding threatened to ruin the rest of our day. It did not because she is quick to anger but quicker to forgive, and Patrick does not hold a grudge at all. Neither of us was wrong in what we did – but Donna was wrong in her reaction.

But what do you do when the misunderstanding is more serious than that? When it becomes personal? How do you prevent yourself from saying words that have to be taken back?

First, you must do what should have been done before the words were spoken – go to God. Ask Him to open the eyes of your understanding, so you can know the truth. Ask Him for a forgiving heart so you can let go of the words said to you or about you. Give Him your repentant heart if your thoughts or words got out of control.

Then sit down as a couple and clear the air. Calm discussion separates the situation from the person. Expressing how the situation made each person feel lets you get the problem off your chests while not making any accusations you might regret later.

Once the situation is diffused, focus on how to avoid the same thing happening again. Look at what started the misunderstanding, and agree to take steps to avoid them. Triggers can be body language, tone of voice, your attitude at the time, or something said by someone else. Identifying it takes the power out of it.

Continue to pray for your spouse. Ask God to reveal where you need to make changes in yourselves. Let God work on the other person, while you love them through the process.

All Wise God, You alone know the beginning from the end. Right now, I am a work in progress. Please give my spouse a patient heart as You continue to work in me, and through me. Amen.

Take-Away for Today

Take some baby oil, and mix some salt in it. Rub it on your spouse's back, and have your spouse rub some on yours. Keep rubbing, a little harder now, until you cannot bear it any more. This is the effect that harsh words and misunderstandings can have on a marriage. A little at a time, you will wear away the gentle love you once knew.

Next, take some baby oil without the salt, and massage each other. Relish the gentle feel of the oil on the skin. Enjoy the intimacy of pleasing your spouse, and do not be surprised that you are pleased in return. Gentle words and a kind touch are good not only for the receiver, but for the giver, as well.

No Matter What

I know what I'm doing. I have it all planned out—plans to take care
of you, not abandon you, plans to give you the future you hope for.
(Jeremiah 29:11 The Message)

Ever notice that the more tired you are, the crankier your
spouse gets? Or the more stress you are under, the more
unreasonable they become?

We were recently working on a job together, and we both
wanted to be finished that day. We were late starting work because
we chose to run some errands first. And to top it off, we were
fighting head colds. In the summer. And it was 90 degrees outside.

We worked together well most of the day with no major
disputes. By late afternoon, though, our nerves began to fray, and
our best behavior coats began to unravel.

All it took was one simple comment out of place, and our
best intentions snapped. And so did we. Luckily, we were alone in
the room with each other, and the television was on in the other
room, so the homeowner did not hear us. We thought no one had
heard us.

But we forgot about the most important One listening. God
heard. We were instantly convicted that this was not the way to
handle the situation. We were embarrassed with ourselves and were
able to patch up our wounded pride.

We were quick to remember that God has good plans for us.
We are to hope in Him, not in our ability to make things work out
according to our schedule. Our future is in Him, not in our ability to
work both ends towards the middle.

When we count on our plans and our abilities, we are
doomed to failure. God created us with a temporary earthly body and
a permanent heavenly mind. The temporary will never achieve the
permanent, and this is where the struggle lies. Counting on our plans

and abilities to make our marriage a success means that we depend entirely on ourselves. When we change our focus from our plans to His, when we aim for God, He will show us His very best

No matter why your first marriage ended, you were not sufficient to meet all the demands, to fulfill all the needs or to supply all the wants and desires of your spouse, your children, your family, your friends, your employer, and any of the hundreds of others who were demanding your attention and energy.

Sure, everyone would like to be Superman or Wonder Woman, able to accomplish everything on our own. But you are not. You need God, because that is how He wants it. You need your spouse, because that's how God designed you. You need each other, because that is the best way to honor and glorify God.

God has wonderful plans for each one as individuals, but He also has great plans for you as a couple. As a remarried couple, you can reach people you could never have reached had you stayed single. You can minister to others in a similar situation that you might never have met had your first marriage not ended. You can testify of God's goodness in finding you a new spouse regardless of how badly you messed up in your previous marriage.

Being a remarried is nothing of which to be ashamed. It is part of God's good plan for you. Embrace it, participate in it, and proclaim it for a world that is longing to hear a word of hope and comfort.

Loving God, thank You for bringing me to this remarriage. Thank You for another chance to show Your love and glory in a dark world. Amen.

Take-Away for Today

If you think your remarriage is not a testimony to the world, consider how much difference a single candle can make. Turn off all the lights in a room at night. Try to read a book and you will see just how dark it is.

Next, light one candle, which represents you. You might be able to read, but it would be difficult.

Light a second candle, which represents you and your spouse and put it near the first one. Now it is much easier to read, but may cause eyestrain after just a short period of time.

Finally, light a third candle, placing it near the first two. Now you cannot only read your book, you can see most of the details of the room.

This is the cumulative effect of you, your spouse, and God, in your marriage. Be a light to the world.

The Greatest Treasure

He will be your safety. He is full of salvation, wisdom, and
knowledge. Respect for the LORD is the greatest treasure.
(Isaiah 33:6 NCV)

We went to the bank to seek out some financing options for
our business. We have operated this business profitably for more
than ten years and have seen it grow beyond our imaginings.
Recently we have seen opportunities for growth that might require
investment, and so we went to see our banker.

We maintain an excellent banking relationship with our bank
and have a very good credit score. We have money in our accounts,
equity in our home, a thriving, if small business, and vehicles that
we don't owe money on. We expected to be approved for our
financing request.

However, the process was not quite as simple as walking in
and just asking for the financing. We had to endure over an hour of
questions regarding our business, our credit, our intended use of the
money, and our ability to repay. Repay? We have always repaid our
debts. How else could we have a good credit score?

Still, the bank had to confirm this information, passing it
through a database of information about us, comparing our potential
for risk to their desire to incur the risk. Then they had to call for
approval. We did get approved, for more than we were asking. There
really was not any doubt about that at all.

Through all of this, we were infinitely glad that we had
maintained a good credit history by faithfully paying all of our bills
on time. We were pleased to learn that because we now owned our
home, the bank was more willing to take a chance with us. And we
saw that our credibility, and credit, were the deciding factors. Not
our intention to repay the money. Not what we were going to do with
the money. It was all based on our credibility.

Sometimes we can tend to treat marriage like a bank loan. We bring our assets and liabilities to the table, and try to balance our relationship using those things that the world looks at. We can create a lot of tension in our marriage by applying our assets and liabilities, our credits and debits, to our relationship with our spouse.

Comparing abilities and weaknesses, past record of blemishes or lack of, and pushing to accomplish and acquire, can all add to the strain. Unrealistic expectations, either for yourself or your spouse, can deplete your energy. Add to that children, family, friends, and jobs, and very soon your precarious house of cards can come tumbling down.

How can you avoid that? Treat your marriage the same way God treats you. When you came to God, you came with nothing. You had no credibility that He could use to determine your worthiness for Him to invest in you. Your hard work was of no matter to God, your family lineage counted for nothing. Even your promise to turn your life around meant nothing at all. God looked at your heart, saw your desire to change, and looked past what you thought was important to what He knows is important.

When you put aside all of the ways to measure success that the world uses, and look instead to how God measures success, you will find hidden treasures in your spouse, your children, and even yourself, that you hadn't seen before. When you apply value to relationships rather than things, you are able to lift and edify those people most important in your lives.

Heavenly Father, thank You for showing me those things of value to You, and for revealing Your love for me through my spouse. Amen.

Take-Away for Today
Focus on people, not on things. Apply value to your relationships, not on your accomplishments. Tonight, before you fall

asleep, tell your spouse ten ways that they showed you today that they love you. Make a habit of doing this each night for the next week. If you have a fight during the day, increase your list to fifteen things.

His Life, Her Life, Our Life

May the God who gives endurance and encouragement
give you a spirit of unity among yourselves
as you follow Christ Jesus.
(Romans 15:5 NIV)

Getting it Together, Together

Always keep yourselves united in the Holy Spirit,
and bind yourselves together with peace.
(Ephesians 4:3 NLT)

Several years ago, we visited the church Donna had attended prior to our marriage. It is a traditional church, well steeped in the proper protocol of when to stand to sing, and when to sit. When the pastor says, "We will stand to sing this next hymn," nobody moves a muscle until the last note of the introduction, when the entire congregation stands up as one.

Patrick, ever the one to break molds, noticed this behavior pattern almost immediately. He has a huge dislike of religious spirits, and so, when the pastor said, "We will stand to sing this next hymn," he stood up right away.

The first time he did it, Donna tugged on his shirtsleeve. He looked down at her as she sat, rooted in her pew. Donna could hear a few snickers from the people seated near her. She could hear what they were thinking. "Doesn't he know how to act in church?" "What kind of a man has she married?" "I thought she said they go to church regularly."

Donna whispered to Patrick, "Not yet." He lifted one eyebrow in question. "Don't stand up yet." She gestured for him to sit. He remained standing. Finally, the last note played, and everyone stood. The second time it happened, she did not try to get his attention. She knew it wouldn't do any good. Instead, she fumed at God. "God, he's embarrassing me!" God spoke loud and clear in her head, "He isn't embarrassing me." What do you say to that? Donna stood. Despite the strange looks she got from the people around her, she stood straight and tall beside her husband.

What embarrasses you doesn't always embarrass God. Patrick was not trying to embarrass Donna or God. He was just doing what came naturally. There is nothing un-Scriptural about standing before the last note of the introduction is played. Donna needed to learn to listen to God and not to religion. She listened and learned an important lesson. When a husband and wife are in unity with each other and with God, they are a mighty force to be reckoned with.

We each bring different backgrounds of faith into our marriage, often different denominations. However, God is clear about headship in the church and the home. God is the head of Jesus, Jesus is the head of man, and man is the head of woman. Any attempt, like Donna tried, to change that, will not please God. Unity in the marriage is paramount to the foundation of the marriage, since marriage is a physical representation of our relationship with God. And unity with God is always the best place to be.

Heavenly Father, thank you for reminding me that together we are stronger, in spite of our differences. You are looking for a unity of purpose, and I thank you for molding me to that purpose. Amen

Take-Away for Today

Take three pieces of wool of different colors, and braid it into a string long enough to tie around your wrist. Wear it proudly as you remember that the colors represent you, your spouse, and God. Together you are stronger and more beautiful.

Keeping it Alive

O God, you are my God, earnestly I seek you;
my soul thirsts for you, my body longs for you,
in a dry and weary land where there is no water.
(Psalm 63:1 NIV)

We go shopping together quite often as a couple. Although we often have different items on our shopping lists, we like to travel as a pair. Generally we split up the shopping list, then meet at the checkout to compare success and bargains. Once in a while, one of us picks up an item that was not on our original list, and so we discuss whether to purchase it or not. Sometimes we find an item that we know was on the other's list.

No matter how long the list, though, inevitably we leave the store with a slightly different selection than we had originally intended. Either we couldn't find something, or we weren't satisfied with the price, or we substituted some other item for it. Maybe we just plain forgot it, even though it was written down. Regardless of why our purchases differed from our original list, you usually treat the experience as a success.

Intimate times with each other should not be treated any differently. Deciding in advance that unless your list is fulfilled, you will not be satisfied, sets you up for failure. Intimate times are not limited to those times behind closed doors. Intimate times include any time you spend alone as a couple.

Watching television or going to a movie are not intimate times. Distractions take away from any discussion that should take place. As a couple, you need regular intimate times where you can talk honestly and openly. The best discussions can happen when you are running on empty and need that time with each other to refresh and renew your marriage. However, it is always better to fill your marriage tank before you run out of gas by giving your marriage priority over anything else that's going on around you.

Many remarrieds find that intimate times are rare. The demands and expectations that you face are often different from those of first-timers. Expectations change, family structures are different, and individual needs have changed from those of first-time marriages.

The main purpose for intimate times in marriage is to cause you to grow closer together as a couple. Closeness builds strength, and a strong marriage can withstand any attacks, from within or without.

In seeking intimate times with each other, do not let the little things get too big, and do not let the big things get out of hand. Deal with the big-ticket items of marriage and relationship as they happen. For example, waiting until the weekend to let your spouse know that you made a mistake in the checkbook and there's an overdraft that will cause your mortgage payment to bounce isn't the wisest thing to do. Alert them when it happens.

Intimacy in your marriage is important because intimacy with God is important. God designed marriage to imitate His relationship with you. As your marriage grows closer, as you learn to love and respect each other more, you find that your relationship with God will grow closer, too.

Heavenly Father, thank you for my spouse. Thank you for this second chance at fulfillment You have given me. When I forget, remind me of the reasons we fell in love. Amen.

Take-Away for Today

Many couples find it difficult to talk openly and honestly. Choose a location and situation where you know you will be alone for a few hours. Turn the lights down low, and sit close to each other.

Have several topics in mind beforehand to talk about. Long-term plans and dreams are good places to start.

Tell your spouse how much they mean to you, how pleased you are with their thoughtfulness. Mention where you see them building strong relationships with others, and pass on a compliment someone else has said about them to you.

This will open the channels for discussion, and soon you will find yourselves looking forward to your discussion times together.

Yield Signs Ahead

Do not be stiff necked, as your fathers were;
submit to the LORD. Come to the sanctuary.
(2 Chronicles 30:8 NIV)

We were waiting in a line for gas a while back. This was a very long line, because the gas station had a special price in honor of a local basketball team's recent victory, reducing the cost of their gas by ninety-four cents a gallon, the number of points the team had scored. And so we waited patiently for over an hour.

Thankfully, before we ran out of things to talk about, a young dog jumped out of a truck three vehicles ahead of us in line. The owner got out with him and threw a Frisbee. The young dog took off after the Frisbee, retrieved it, and brought it back to the truck. Or almost.

He stopped about ten feet from the truck and dropped the Frisbee. The owner patiently pointed to the Frisbee repeatedly, trying to show the dog to pick it up and bring it all the way to him.

The dog would pick it up, take a few steps, then drop it. Repeatedly this went on, creating a funny diversion. Finally, the dog brought the Frisbee to the owner's feet and dropped it there. The man picked up the Frisbee and threw it again. The dog retrieved it, bringing the disc closer this time before dropping it about five feet from the owner.

Once again, the young man patiently went through the process of coaxing the dog to bring the Frisbee closer. Once again, the dog eventually understood, and the Frisbee was tossed again for him.

Over the course of the next forty minutes, the dog learned that when he brought the Frisbee right to his owner's feet, the game continued much more quickly, as the disc was thrown more often.

When this finally clicked in its understanding, the puppy brought the Frisbee directly to his owner's feet. Where at first the dog did not understand what was expected of him, its understanding was completed in its obedience.

Marriage is often a battle of two wills. In particular, people who have been married before bring a different set of understandings into the marriage. These understandings may be shaped by the previous marriage relationships – by the things that worked, and by the things that did not. You can be emotionally hurt by how you were treated inside the marriage, and by how you were treated when the marriage ended.

Especially difficult can be a Christian marriage because of the concepts of submission and obedience. The first requirement for husbands and for wives is to submit to God, to be obedient to Him. Secondly, the scriptural requirement is for wives to submit to their husbands as their husband is submitting to and obeying God.

It is easy to confuse submission with subjection. Subjection implies the stronger forcing the weaker to a position of servitude. God never does this with you, so do not think He wants you to do it with each other. Submission, on the other hand, implies putting the other person's needs and desires before your own.

Just as a parent knows what is best for their children and instructs them in the safe and proper way, so does God for you. He has set up marriage as an example of your relationship with Him. Submission is a tough concept that has been misused in the past. True godly submission is a place of safety, of putting the other person first. In fact, true submission is the greatest demonstration of love possible. There is no better way to show your love for God than to do as He asks.

In marriage, if wives can love their husbands the way they love God, and if husbands love their wives enough to put aside their own agenda and desires, there will be no clashing of wills. As each seeks to grow in relationship with God, your marriage relationship will grow and improve.

Your ultimate goal with God is to obey and submit to Him from desire and without thought; God's desire is that you treat each other the same way.

Loving God, work in me and through me today as You create in me a heart of submission and a desire for You. Amen.

Take-Away for Today

Remember the three-legged races from your school days? Tie a belt or band around your left ankle and around your spouse's right ankle. Don't hold on to each other in any way, don't communicate where you want to go – each just try to go about your own plans.

You will quickly find that much energy goes into trying to make the other person conform to your desires. The stronger or more persistent will eventually win, but the result will be that the stronger will then have to drag the other person around, because that person is tired by the exertion. This is an example of subjection and servitude.

Then, link arms, and decide where you will go together. If each is to accomplish their goals, you will have to compromise at times, and sometimes you will have to defer. However, less energy is spent getting done what you want, attitudes will be better, and more will get done. This is an example of submission – yielding to the other's desires for the benefit of both.

Whose Friend are You?

Abraham believed God, and that faith was regarded
by God to be his approval of Abraham.
So Abraham was called God's friend.
(James 2:23 God's Word)

We have a friend who is getting married again soon. She is divorced, and he is a widower. They have been seeing each other for several months, and have a number of friends in common already. However, they also discovered during their wedding plans that they each have a separate circle of friends from 'before'.

As a remarried, you know what we mean. Friends who knew you when you were married to someone else. Friends with a set of memories about you that doesn't include your current spouse. Friends who know things about your previous marriage that you might not want to share with your new love.

How you handle this will set the tone for the future of your marriage. If you try to keep these friendships separate, you might find it is like living a double life. In one life, there are 'our' friends, and in the other life, there are 'my' friends and 'your' friends. It gets difficult to remember whom you told what to, and how much you told them. In some ways, it will be like starting a lie – keeping the stories straight.

In God's perfect plan, marriage would be forever, and we'd never have to be concerned about meshing the past, present, and future of two people more than once. Because if you remember back, it was hard enough the first time around. And that was before either one had a lot of history.

But we don't always live in God's perfect plan. In our lives, there are second and subsequent marriages to deal with. New friends to be made, old friendships to be consolidated into the marriage.

God desires above all that you live in relationship with Him – He is to be your best friend. Second to Him, your spouse is to be your best friend. Any time you get that out of order, there are bound to be conflicts. To have a friend, be a friend.

To be a friend to God and to your spouse takes three things – time, time, and time. Just as you build a house brick upon brick, you build your relationship with God word upon word, precept upon precept. Just as you get to know a person by listening and asking questions, you develop a deep friendship with your spouse by listening and talking. Spending time together. Finding common likes and dislikes.

This does not mean that every waking minute must be spent with your spouse. It does mean that God should be the first thought you have in the morning and the last at night. It means that no matter where you are or what we're doing, do it as if God and your spouse were right there with you. Preface every decision with "What do God and my spouse think about this? How does this benefit them?"

Thinking of God and your spouse as primary relationships in your life will cause them to become the primary relationships. When measured against them, your other friendships should pale in comparison. When a conflict arises, the decision should be an easy one – God first, your spouse second. That includes knowing that sometimes it is best for everyone if a friendship is allowed to lapse into acquaintanceship and sometimes even allowed to fall by the wayside. Once the decision is made, the outcome is assured.

Having God call you His friend is your life's goal as a Christian. Being your spouse's best friend brings honor to both of you. The world would tell you there are many reasons why you should not be best of friends – look for the reasons why you should be.

God, thank you for being a friend to me when I was unfriendly. Thank You for loving me when I was unloving. Change me to hunger for Your friendship. Amen.

Take-Away for Today

Make a list of all the people you consider friends. Then estimate how much time you spend with each one. Consider their lifestyles and marriage relationships. Do they honor God, lift up their spouse, and live a life you would be proud to call your own? Or would you be embarrassed to bring them to your mother's house for dinner? Are there any friends that are not mutual to you and your spouse? Have an honest discussion with your spouse about your feelings, and see if there are any people you should spend less time with, or some with whom you should spend more time.

Prayers of Agreement

When a believing person prays, great things happen.
(James 5:16 NCV)

You have probably noticed that a child's attention span is very short. What is amazing, however, is that this Short Attention Span Syndrome, or SASS, is very selective. Kids can sit for hours in a movie theater and never budge, whereas they cannot sit for ten minutes in church.

They can lie on their backs on the grass and see pictures in the clouds for hours, and not be able to get comfortable in their bed at night to sleep. And, of course, don't forget they can pass a popsicle around a group and be able to keep track of whose turn it is and who had the most, but they cannot remember that the trash cans go on the curb every Thursday.

Attention span is very much dictated by what else is going on around you. Even as an adult, you find those things you enjoy doing can be done for interminable hours. And so, what is wrong with that? Nothing, so long as those things that grab your attention and hold it for long periods of time are beneficial to your relationship with God and with your spouse.

One very important area in your relationship with God and your spouse is your prayer life. Time spent in prayer serves several purposes. First, it humbles you to admit that you need help, and second, it points you to the only One who is able to solve all your problems, God.

Admitting that you cannot solve all your problems and supply all of your needs and all of your wants is a big first step. Admitting that to your spouse is the next step. Going to God with your spouse and admitting that you cannot change them is the key to opening the blessings that God has in store for you.

Praying with your spouse allows them to see that private side that you keep hidden from the world. It also allows you a glimpse into their private side. After all, a marriage is the combining of two separate people into one person in God, and so joining in prayer is the next logical step.

When you first make the commitment to pray together as a couple, you might find it uncomfortable. Many times your prayer languages can be different. Depending on how you were taught to pray, you may tend to speak in King James English. Others tend to free flow ramble as thought come to you. Still others might use a list or a prayer chart.

No matter how you pray, or what position you take when you pray, the important thing is that you want to pray together. Decide ahead of time that there will be no snickering, no rolling of eyes, no judgmental attitude allowed in your prayer time. Choose a time when you are less likely to be disturbed. When the children are living at home, it is a good idea to pray with your children in family prayer time, but also be sure to set aside some couple prayer time as well.

Couple prayer time and family prayer time should not take away from your private prayer time. Personal time spent with God is like the time an athlete spends in working out. No matter how much they practice, they still need to spend time on specific endurance and strength exercises. Personal prayer time is your personal workout, couple prayer time is your pre-game pep talk, family prayer time is your practice, and how you apply what you learn during prayer time is the actual game.

Yes, you should learn something during prayer time. Prayer is not just a shopping list of wants and needs that God answers. Prayer time is also a time of seeking direction, asking for help in a particular area of your faith walk, and a time of repentance in areas of your life where you messed up. During prayer time, you should be listening for God's direction at least half of the time. After all, how can you hear from God unless you stop talking?

There are a great many distractions in our lives that pull us away from time spent with God. There will always be one more chore to finish, one more call to make, one more project that just cannot wait. However, if we choose to put God first in our marriage and our lives, we will find that these other tasks become much easier. God wants to hear from us , and He desires to give us all those good things He has in store for us, including answered prayer.

Lord, I know I don't spend enough time listening to You. Forgive me for my laundry list of needs, and silence my tongue to hear You. Amen.

Take-Away for Today
Commit to spending 10 minutes each day with your spouse in prayer. Each of you make a list of things to pray about, and when you come together to pray, compare lists.

For the first week of this new adventure, cross off any items that are on both lists. You can pray for those in your personal prayer time. Pray as a couple for the unique items on both lists. In the second week, pray as a couple for those items that are only on both lists, while you pray for the unique items on your own list during your personal prayer time. Alternate the unique and duplicated items prayer format, one week at a time.

His Friends, Her Friends, Our Friends

In my early years, the friendship of God was felt in my home.
(Job 29:4 NLT)

Times of Refreshing

The generous prosper and are satisfied;
those who refresh others will themselves be refreshed.
(Proverbs 11:25 NLT)

It is amazing how God can bring together two seemingly different personalities and expect them to become one in Him. As an example, Donna is a list person. She makes lists of the things she wants to do today, and then gauges how well her day went by how many items she checked off. Her theory is 'if it was important enough to write down, it is important enough to do.' Patrick, however, is a fly-by-the-seat-of-his-pants kind of guy. His theory is 'if it doesn't get done, it did not need to get done today'.

Needless to say, we are often at loggerheads about what is the most important thing to accomplish in a given time frame. And that can lead to conflict.

It can be very easy to spend so much time focusing on the day-to-day activities that we forget about the reason for doing a certain thing. As an example, if Donna has 'laundry' on her list for today, is it important that it be done today? It is, if we expect to go on vacation tomorrow, and need clean clothes to put in the suitcase. On the other hand, most of the time there is no reason why laundry cannot be delayed one more day.

We are not promoting procrastination in any way. We are promoting flexibility, something which many have a problem with. When we focus on the 'what' instead of the 'why', we can easily miss the boat. Flexibility allows us to be able to change our priorities as the situation around us changes, so that we aren't stressed by the unexpected.

Focusing on the 'what' takes our eyes off the big picture and on to the details. It can also lead to distraction and frustration, and tends to bring the focus on to 'me' and my needs. Such nearsightedness causes us to take our eyes off God and each other. We forget that we are part of a team in our marriage, and we forget the reason why we married in the first place.

We are not a team of one. We are part of a team of three – God, our spouse, and us. In that order. Marriage, jobs, children, family, and recreation all demand our time and energy. Often, at the end of the day, when we climb into bed, we are so exhausted we just want to go to sleep.

Not only does our intimate life suffer, but also our relationship as a whole can deteriorate. When we do not spend time with each other on a regular basis, we can lose touch with the person we first fell in love with.

Our relationship with God is much the same. When we don't spend time with Him on a regular basis, we lose touch of His will and purpose for our life. A big part of His purpose for our life is fellowship with Him. Another part is our fellowship with brothers and sisters in Christ. Focusing on our needs, our desires, and our list takes our eyes off others.

So take your eyes off the list and instead, ask God what He wants done today. Ask your spouse what they want to do. Then look around for opportunities to be the refreshing moment that someone else needs today.

Loving God, thank You that You are bigger than my list, bigger than my wants and desires. Show me how You would use me today, for Your glory. Amen.

Take-Away for Today

Sit down as a couple and each make a list of the things you would like to do together as a couple and as a family. Then cross off any items that are on both lists, and schedule time to do those things that are only on one list.

Companionable Silence

The LORD is in his holy temple;
let all the earth be silent before him.
(Habakkuk 2:20 NIV)

We recently visited a small tourist town in the off-season. We don't know what this place is normally like although based on the number of restaurants, ski shops, and snowboard rental shops within a two city block area that we walked one rainy day, we think that town is bustling during ski season.

On this particular day, however, all of the shops were closed – 'end of season' and 'R&R break' signs were posted in many windows. Some said when they would re-open, but most did not. It probably depends on when it turns cold and the snow machines can be started up for the winter again. Several businesses that catered to more than the snow sport crowd, such as restaurants, art galleries, and souvenir shops, would reopen in the summer. Many were closed from March until September or October.

We walked hand in hand along the boardwalk, peering through windows into darkened stores, pointing out the wares you could see, gasping in delight at the exorbitant prices.

And then we walked along quietly, taking in the breathtaking scenery around us, looking up the mountain at the ski runs turning green with new growth, imagining the crowds at the ski lifts, glad we were here now, in the silence.

Everyone has busy lives, working at a variety of jobs, wearing many different hats on a daily basis. There is seldom time to go for a walk in our normal lives, although we know we should. There is rarely time for an afternoon nap, or to sit around staring into the fireplace.

It seems that in the busyness of our lives, we lose connectedness with one another. Sometimes in all that busyness, we can even lose connection with God. We get distracted by what we feel we need to accomplish, by the needs of others around us, and by our own needs.

Contrary to popular opinion, much can be accomplished in the silence. Silence encourages us to search ourselves, to make changes to what we don't like, and to repeat what we do like.

Silence and solitude can lead us to a deeper realization of God and His will in our lives. Silence causes us to listen more and to talk less. We can learn only when we listen, and everyone has much to learn from God, although our culture has taught us there is something wrong with silence.

There is nothing inherently wrong with silence. Just like money, silence is a tool, to be used for a purpose. And we can choose whether we use it for good or for bad. Money can be used for bad purposes when it is placed before people in our lives, when the pursuit of money becomes our primary goal, or when it is used to control people. In the same way, silence is being used for wrong purposes when we selfishly put our desire for solitude above anything else, when we avoid doing anything else, or when we use it to punish those around us .

In marriage, silence and solitude can bring restoration to a broken relationship. Silence can bring about reconciliation in a strained relationship. Silence can result in renewal of our first loves, God and our spouse, in that order.

To experience this restoration, reconciliation, and renewal we must be willing to focus on each other and on God. Focusing on our spouse causes us to take your mind off our own agenda, and to see our spouse through a different perspective. When we do that, we will see aspects of our spouse we never knew before.

In the same way, focusing on God will show us different aspects of Him and His character that we never knew before. God speaks loudly through the silences. He is that 'small still voice' that guides and directs. He will guide and direct our life, if we give Him the chance.

Patient Lord, thank You for wanting to spend time with me and with my spouse. We invite You to show us how to be silent before You, so that in the silence we may hear You loud and clear. Amen

Take-Away for Today

Even if you cannot find the time or resources to remove yourself physically as a couple from your environment, you can create a place of silence and solitude. You do not have to 'go away' for a week or even a weekend. These retreats are a wonderful bonus, but you can 'get away' for an hour a week.

Turn off the phone, the television, the computer. Send the kids to bed a little early if need be. Turn off the lights, and retreat to your bedroom. Begin your time together with prayer, as you seek God, asking Him to reveal himself to you, through you, and for you.

Set a timer not to speak for five minutes. When the timer goes off, set it again for five minutes – then talk about whatever it was that God brought to your mind. Stop when the timer goes off again. At first, this will seem like a strange way to spend an hour with your spouse. Sitting quietly will be foreign. You will each be tempted to speak about things that come to mind from the activities of the day.

Repeat this process for the hour or so that you have set aside. Don't worry if there are things you did not get a chance to say – this will give you a reason to repeat this retreat time again soon.

Give and Take

Each of you should give whatever you have decided.
You shouldn't be sorry that you gave or feel forced to give,
since God loves a cheerful giver.
(2 Corinthians 9:7 God's Word)

Some would tell you that a successful marriage is a game of give and take. 50-50. Right down the middle. They are right but they are also wrong. Marriage is a give and take, but it is by no means 50-50.

Marriage is give 100% and expect to take nothing. When you marry for 50-50, you will spend half your time working for the half you hope to get. Unfortunately, what you get will probably disappoint you from time to time.

To avoid disappointment, make up your mind now, today, that instead of looking for ways to get, you will look for ways to give. Instead of seeking your pleasure, seek to please your spouse. Rather than ask 'what's in it for me?' ask 'how much of me can I give you?'

If you find yourself seeking after your own satisfaction too often, and your spouse looks to their own satisfaction, your marriage relationship will suffer. To have a best friend in your spouse, you must be a best friend. Developing a close relationship requires time, commitment, honesty, and trust.

Your relationship with God is the same. If you seek a deeper relationship with God for what He can give you and do for you, you are missing out. While God will do and give, His primary desire is for you, personally.

God did not choose you as a couple to be a part of His family because of what you can do for Him or give Him. He chose you because He loves you. He chose you because He wants to be best friends with you, and because He wants to spend time with you.

As you spend time with God, you discover aspects of His character that you never knew. Building a deeper relationship with Him will strengthen your faith, bolster your resolve, and improve your marriage.

Primarily, seek God for who He is, and He will reveal His love for you in ways you never imagined. As God demonstrates his love for you, ask Him to show how to show that love to your spouse.

Giving of yourself unconditionally is liberating. You are able to expend your energies without concern about how it will be returned to you . In some ways, it is like investing money in a worthy cause without knowing what the interest rate is and without caring. The investment is the reward.

Lord, forgive me for not putting You first in my life. Forgive me for not treating You and my spouse the way You treat me. Show me Your way. Amen.

Take-Away for Today

Invest in your marriage today. Do something nice for your spouse, something unexpected, something you know they have longed for. It does not have to be something you buy or somewhere you go. You do not need to spend money, unless your money is the thing you have been holding back. Think of ways to spend time together if you are a workaholic. If your children have been the barrier, send them to a neighbor's house for a sleepover, and spend an evening or weekend alone with your spouse. If habits, such as TV, crafts, or sports have driven a wedge between you, hide the remote control and cancel all other appointments for the day.

While this may seem like a huge sacrifice, remember – your spouse is going to be looking for ways to give to you too. Imagine the fun you will have!

In the Garden

The LORD will comfort Israel again and make her deserts blossom.
Her barren wilderness will become as beautiful as Eden—
the garden of the LORD. Joy and gladness will be found there.
Lovely songs of thanksgiving will fill the air.
(Isaiah 51:3 NLT)

There are just as many kinds of gardens as there are people. We recently visited the local Botanic Gardens, a trip we like to make at least a couple of times a year. However, we had gotten way too busy, and realized as we walked the pathways that it had been two years since we had been there last.

Needless to say, there were a lot of changes in that time. A favorite of Donna's, the rose garden, was not where it had been. The herb garden, which had been under construction on our previous visit, was now thriving and vibrant. We enjoyed looking at all the different herbs, most of them foreign to us, noting their uses as ornamental, cooking, or medicinal.

On and on we walked, admiring God's amazing variety and imagination in His creation. From time to time, Patrick commented out loud, as much for the benefit of the people standing nearby as for Donna's, about how loving God must be to surround us with so much beauty. In one of the mini-gardens, we found a plaque with a scripture and prayer, the first evidence of someone else recognizing the truth of where all this beauty came from.

Still, there were some plants and arrangements that did not appeal to us. Milk thistle was growing in one area, with some of the plants bearing those awful thorned pods that stick in your clothes if you walk too close to it. In another area, there was a beautiful tree covered with flowers, but the flowers smelled like rotten meat. Not our idea of a nice perfume.

Some of the plants had already flowered and were now into the fruit-producing stage, while many plants were just now blooming. There were grasses that did not ever bear flowers, trees that grew twenty-five feet in one year, and plants that only bloom every ten years or so.

So much variety, all gathered in one place, all designed, and created, by the same God. Thousands of volunteers and workers maintain these gardens, a lot of work and money is invested, and many people go to look at these plants, getting ideas for their own gardens, or just to admire and marvel.

Still, as in any garden, there were some weeds present. We saw many workers pulling plants that were growing where they shouldn't be, and we saw them trimming away dead branches and pulling dead flower heads. There were even several areas where the weeds had overtaken the planned growth, and so the weeds and the planned growth were torn up, weed killer was liberally applied, and the area was being 'weed proofed' before new plants were put in.

As we walked the pathways, as we stood in the shade of arbors or sat on the bench near the lily pond, we saw God in every turn. The Lord of the Universe invested a lot of thought in what He created. Some of the plants would not have been our choice, like the milk thistle or the stinky flower tree. Still, God has a purpose for them in His plan.

Just as He has a purpose in your remarriage. Sometimes you might find that there are a few weeds in your marriage that you did not plant there, and you don't want them there. Maybe it is just a hint of a rotten smell, or maybe the pods are sticking to you because you've gotten too close to them. Whatever it is, no matter how long it is been there, it is time to get rid of it.

Weeds can even be disguised as pretty plants that are just growing in the wrong place. For example, marigolds in the middle of a petunia bed will take away from the effect you are trying to accomplish in the petunia bed. In the same way, a weed called gossip can easily grow where you may have been trying to plant care and concern over a friend's behavior.

If you decide to nip those weeds in the bud, to plant only what you want to grow where you want it to grow, and then nourish it with the love of God, with Jesus the Living Water and the Bread of Life, then your garden – your remarriage – will grow and flourish, a testimony to others around you .

Loving Creator, thank You for the beauty around me. Now, bring that beauty into me as You change me into Your likeness and image. Show me how to allow others to grow, too. Amen.

Take-Away for Today

Your remarriage is like a garden, so treat it like one. Get some books from the library on planning a garden that will thrive in your area. Whether you have a piece of land or you decide to use containers or planters, think about what you would like to grow. Choose flowers, plants, fruit, or vegetables. Discuss this as a couple, and consider the following questions:

How big do you want this garden to be?

How many people can you get involved to help you ?

How much time do you want to spend each day, each week, each month?

Do you want a quick harvest, a bountiful harvest, or an ongoing harvest?

What will you do with the produce of your garden?

How do you plan to limit and eliminate weeds?

As you think about your options for your garden, think also about your options for your remarriage. When you think of your remarriage as a living, growing entity, you will see that some planning and precautions may be necessary. Take action, enjoy the growth, and then sit back and wonder at the harvest.

His Baggage, Her Baggage, Our Future

There is indeed a future, and your hope will never be cut off.
(Proverbs 23:18 ASV)

Surrounded by History

I will remember the deeds of the LORD.
I will remember your ancient miracles.
(Psalm 77:11 NAS)

A local courthouse displays mementoes of its namesake, a local judge. Things that were once new and shiny to its original owner are now tattered and dusty. A sword belonging to a grandfather, a gun used in the Civil War, a college jersey with moth holes carefully concealed in the folds, even the chair he sat on in his courtroom. What once was of use is now on display. This building, originally built as a post office, was later converted into a courthouse. A number of years ago, millions of dollars spent to restore the building to its original design.

History costs you. You can choose to put your history to work for you, like this old building, by teaching you important lessons, or you can let it control you and weigh you down. History can be a good thing, where you learn from past mistakes, where you grow in your relationship with God, and where you become a better spouse.

Your past relationships created history in you as individuals, a history of experiences and lessons learned that you bring into your new marriage, and this history can either weigh you down or lift you up.

Sometimes you have to choose to let your history go. When it causes you to repeat mistakes, or it interferes with your marriage or your relationship with God, you must release it so you can be released to experience the best God has for you.

God's plans for you include creating a new future. What you surround yourselves with will determine the direction you take. Just like this old building commemorates the life experiences of its namesake, your lives commemorate what you choose.

Are you choosing positive experiences that build you up and cause you to make better choices, or do you surround yourselves in history that tears down and causes you to make choices that impede your marriage?

It can be hard to let go of the past. After all, your past is a big part of who you are. For many, your past contains the badges you wear proudly that set you apart and make you special, even if in a negative way.

Just like this old building, remodeling your lives can be expensive, disruptive, and even painful. Those things that worked for you before are now detrimental to your marriage. Old habits and patterns need to be exchanged for new.

Working out your new marriage is like the remodeling process. There will be trash to throw out. There will be lots of dust and debris. There will even be some things that will not come out unless they are broken.

You know and trust that God is the ultimate interior designer. He knows exactly what the finished product will look like, because He knows the beginning from the end. He can call you beautiful and complete and finished, because that is what He sees. Just like when you decide to paint a room in your house, you can envision what it will look like when done, God sees you as a perfect complete package.

Choose to let go of anything that holds you back from being all that God has planned for you. That includes the hurts of past relationships. That also includes your accomplishments, your successes, and your badges of honor, even the negative ones, like abandoned, abused, or cheated on. Choose also to let go of whatever has already happened to hurt you in this remarriage.

When you carry history over to your new marriage, you begin to look for repeated mistakes in others. If you have seen the past in your new spouse, ask God for His vision. He sees perfection in you and in your spouse.

The past can hurt you only if you choose to repeat it. Your history is gone and over, and any part you had in it is forgiven through the grace and mercy of a God who has cast it as far as the east is from the west. You can decide to do the same, and cut your spouse – and yourselves – some slack.

Loving God, forgive me for wearing badges that are not from You. Forgive me for clinging to the past, and show me the future You have for me. Amen.

Take-Away for Today

On small pieces of paper, write down those hurts and wrongs from the past that you don't want to bring into your remarriage. Then take them outside and burn them, or bury them, or tear them into tiny pieces and toss them into the wind, never to be recalled again.

Then write down on index cards all the ways your spouse and your new marriage have blessed you. Tape, pin, or place them in prominent places around your home, such as on mirrors, over doors, in the bathroom, over the kitchen sink. Tuck a few into favorite books to be found later, or into your spouse's sock drawer.

My Stuff, Your Stuff

Get for yourselves purses that will not wear out,
the treasure in heaven that never runs out,
where thieves cannot steal and moths cannot destroy.
Your heart will be where your treasure is.
(Luke 12:33-34 NCV)

When we first discussed getting married, there were many things to consider. First, we wanted to know for sure if this was God's will, because if it was not, we knew it would fail. Secondly, we wanted our pastor's approval of the marriage, because he knew Patrick better than Donna did, and he did not know Donna at all.

We had already had long conversations about God, our faith, our individual theology, and the direction our marriage would take. We had done several Bible studies together, and felt we knew each other fairly well.

Then came the discussions about actually combining our households. We both had considerable 'stuff', not all of it useful or necessary. Add to that the fact that Donna had to ship her stuff over three thousand miles, which added to the difficulty of what to choose. Economics would dictate not to ship anything that could be bought for less than the shipping costs. Still, sentimentality often overrides economics.

What we discovered about each other during these discussions of our stuff was our polar opposite definition of what was important and what was not. Patrick has no concept of the intrinsic value of mementoes, while Donna does not 'get' the point of having two irons, in case one breaks down. After all, if one breaks, either fix it or throw it away and buy a new one, right?

Not so with Patrick. He figures so long as it is smaller than an oversized breadbox, keeping it will not make a difference to our storage. Donna's point is, if you keep an extra of everything, soon your storage will be so full you cannot find anything anyway. On the other hand, Patrick felt that mementoes, like a vase that Donna's grandmother had given her when she was 16, could, and should, be done away with, because it serves no useful purpose.

Useful purpose? Does everything have to serve a useful purpose? Can't you cherish something, not because of what it is, but because of who gave it to you?

What Donna found out during this moving process was that what you own can start to own you. She had a pair of gloves, for example, that her mother gave her a year or so before she'd died. Donna had worn them out, and then stored them away in a closet because she could not bear to throw them out. After all, her mother had given them to her. She could not wear them anymore, because there were more holes than leather left, but still....

As Donna pondered the economics and the sentiments of what to take with her, she came to realize that she was not honoring her mother by keeping those gloves in a closet, or in a drawer, or in a box in storage. Donna honored her mother by her life, by living as she lived, by honoring Patrick as her mom had honored her husband, Donna's father.

Patrick, a complete opposite when it came to mementoes, realized that his disposition of most of his belongings several years before had been done under the false assumption that to have things meant his trust was in things. In an effort to maintain his faith and trust only in God, he had discarded items that belonged to his mother and grandmother, items that were useful or valuable, or both. He saw that it was not the fact that he had gotten rid of them that was wrong, but rather the manner.

We were relieved to see that we were not alone in our feelings about our belongings. Since then, we have seen similar situations when there is remarriage. Regardless of why the marriage ended, through either divorce or death, each person has a different reaction. You might want to get rid of anything that reminds you of the former spouse, or hold onto the memory of that other person through things.

One way to handle the memory-keeping situation is to move to a new home, one that can belong to your remarriage, one not shared by the former spouse. Set out the duplicates you are bringing into the marriage, and decide which one to keep, based on its usefulness and condition. By setting it out in the new home, you remove any sentimentality that may have been attached to it before. This is also a good opportunity to divide some things amongst the children and other family members who might like a keepsake or two.

If, on the other hand, you are coming into your remarriage with virtually nothing, do not feel as if you need to replace all of it at once. Remind yourselves that this stuff is not permanent. If you do not get your dream dishes right now, you can always get them later.

When you put aside the importance of things, you see that in your walk of faith with God, you can choose to keep and honor mementoes and traditions, or you can honor Him. In your remarriage, you can choose to honor your idea of the perfect spouse, or you can honor your spouse, as they are. And honor does not require things. Honor requires action.

So rather than argue with your spouse about the value of having two of everything, instead honor them, and your marriage, and God. Because when all is said and done, all the stuff in the world won't make you happy. Only God can do that.

God, forgive me for putting so much value in things that I sometimes neglect my relationship with You. Show me how to let go of the things of this world, and to seek You alone. Amen.

Take-Away for Today

As a couple, go through one closet or one stuffed dresser, and decide, as a couple, what to keep, what to give away, and what to throw out. Do this at least every six months, and find out what is important to your spouse, and why. Make sure neither ridicules or belittles the other for their feelings about an object, whether they want to keep it or toss it. Consider what you might give to your children or save for them for when they are older.

For Better or For Worse

A man leaves father and mother and is firmly bonded to his wife,
becoming one flesh—no longer two bodies but one.
(Matthew 19:5 The Message)

Getting married is one of the most exciting days in anyone's life. You eagerly look forward to your future together, making plans, anticipating the years ahead. You recite your vows, you enjoy the congratulations of friends and family, and you really don't see beyond today. You believe that everything is going to be good and fun and happy. You believe you are going to be loved, and have enough money, and live long enough to enjoy many happy years together, retiring in good health, and growing old together.

And then comes the reality of everyday living. Questions like 'who cleans the toilet?' or 'who balances the check book' suddenly become major battle zones. This perfect person you married who kept an immaculate home morphs into a slob overnight. The calm rational person you married is suddenly transformed into Dr. Jekyll and Mr. Hyde.

Face it – the courtship is over, and real life begins. Where once you were willing to do whatever it took to convince your spouse that you are the perfect one for them, now you find those annoying little habits are, well, annoying.

How did this happen? To begin with, you were on your best behavior during the courtship process, and no matter how honest you intended to be with your intended, you were still not showing them the real you. After all, you care about this person, and you do not want to scare them off, right?

But now that you're married, it is hard to keep up the facade day in and day out. You have other things on your mind, big things, like, who's going to clean the toilet?

God designed marriage to join two people to make them one.

Note that the word 'join' is used here. God did not intend to melt you together, to mash you together, or even to make you the same.

He joins you, like a sailor joins two pieces of rope. Sometimes one kind of rope just will not do the whole job. For example, nylon rope withstands salt water, but can be slippery when it gets wet. As a result, a sailor might choose to join a piece of nylon rope for use below the water line, to a piece of cotton rope that is going to be used in the rigging. Joining two pieces of rope, especially when they are not the same kind of rope, can be a tricky situation. Joining them with a knot will cause the knot to slip. Applying a flame to melt the nylon to the cotton will burn the cotton, making it useless.

The best way to join two pieces of rope that are not made of the same material is to unwind one end of each rope, and then braid them together. This creates a bond, a three-strand cord, which is not easily broken, just as scripture says. The join is strong, there is no knot to get tangled in, and there are no burnt ends.

God joins you together in much the same way. He intertwines you, using Himself as the central cord in the braid. When you are intertwined with God and your spouse, nothing will be able to tangle you, pull you apart, or cause you to unravel.

When your marriage is strong, God can use you more in His plans. You can be a role model for others around you and a testimony to just how good God is. After all, if He can take two opposites and make them one through Him, He is truly a God of Miracles!

Lord, show us how to be one in You, and how to show that to a world that seeks role models. Let others see You, not us, in all you do. Amen.

Take-Away for Today

Take a piece of wool, and pull hard on it to test its strength. Then, take three pieces and braid them into a single cord. Now pull hard on this to see how strong it is. This three-cord strand can withstand much more pressure than the single strand. You, your spouse, and God form a strong cord that is not easily broken. Keep the braided strand handy, so that when you feel like life is unraveling, you can remind yourself of just how strong your marriage is in God.

Overwhelming Baggage

"Remember the old days. Think of the years already passed.
Ask your father and he will tell you;
ask your older leaders and they will inform you."
(Deuteronomy 32:7 NCV)

Before reading this, go out and look at the family car. Yes, that sounds like a funny thing to say, in preparation for reading a devotional. Go and look at the car. Look closely at it. See the little bug splatters on the headlights? The tiny dents from sand and gravel on your windshield? Maybe there are a few dings from other car doors, or a major bump in a fender from an inconsiderate shopping cart.

Some of the marks may even be of something you did. You scratched your car by pulling a box across the trunk lid, or by chipping at ice and hitting the roof instead. Maybe your car is like yours and looks like it was driven though a sand storm too many times. Even if your car is brand new, there are probably some chips in the paint down near the wheel wells.

It is practically impossible to drive a car without getting some damage, even if you cannot see it unless we're looking for it.

Life is like that, too. As you go through life experiences, you pick up small dents and dings that are invisible to the naked eye. You go through fender-benders and major wrecks, each one leaving its own scars. Broken relationships, lost opportunities, friendships neglected, love lost – all have an impact and can leave you scarred and broken.

And then you get married. You bring those scars and broken parts into your marriage. And when that marriage ends, you add new scars and damage to what you already had. And then you get married again.

How can you break this cycle of bringing overwhelming baggage into your new marriage? You can read all the self-help books you want, go to all the counseling sessions you can afford, and still have those scars.

The only truly permanent way to do plastic surgery on your past scars is to give them up. Make the choice that you will not carry this baggage around with you anymore. It doesn't matter whether the scar is because of something you did to yourselves, or whether you were a victim of another person or situation – you have the choice of whether to retain ownership.

Choosing not to claim that scar is not an easy thing. It is not merely as simple as saying, for example, "I will not get angry when my spouse forgets my birthday." Choose and refuse – you decide you don't want to live under the curse of the past and resist any attempt of the enemy to make you forget that decision.

Choose and refuse – when the past comes back to haunt you, you must first remind yourselves of your decision not to be subjected to the past. Then go to God, asking for the strength to resist. When you are able to give the past to God, He is much more able to take care of it. He is then released to deal with it in a righteous way. When you retain ownership of the past, you prevent God from handling it for you.

Choose and refuse – as many times as it takes to relinquish control to God. As many times as the enemy reminds you of a past mistake or a past hurt, you must give it to God. That could be many times a day at first. But you can be sure that God is faithful, and He will provide a way through.

So whether it is dealing with anger at your spouse, or controlling some aspect of your behavior, such as a bad habit, give it to God. Choose and refuse – and watch your marriage flourish.

Heavenly Father, You know my heart. Search it. Reveal to me those areas that You need to deal with. I cannot do it on my own. Amen.

Take-Away for Today

Take a walk with your spouse in an area where you can pick up small rocks. A beach is a good place, but a country path, a park walkway, and even your own neighborhood will do.

Each choose a small rock that has a lot of cracks, chips, and flaws in it. The find one that is perfectly smooth. Use the flawed rock to remind you of what you used to be like. Use the smooth rock to show you where you are headed in your marriage, in your relationships, and in your walk with God.

If possible, choose a larger version of each to place in a prominent spot in your home, such as on a coffee table or shelf, or in your own garden. Use it to testify to others of the growth in your marriage and your relationship with the Lord.

All the Time in the World

*You may work for six days, but the seventh day is a day of worship,
a day when you don't work. It is holy to the LORD.*
(Exodus 31: 15 NAS)

Since every remarried has been married before, it only stands to reason that you're older than you used to be. When you were younger, your focus was on getting a job, buying a house, and raising kids. Now that you're older, your focus tends to change. Now you look forward to paying off the house, or moving into a smaller one. You may be paying for college tuition, or vacation homes. Maybe you're looking forward to grandchildren, or even great grandchildren.

No matter what your family status, one thing is closer to you now than when you were younger – retirement. Most people have visions of what your retirement will look like. For some, travel to exotic places is high on their wish list. For others, weeks at the cabin in the mountains, or the lake house, or on a houseboat somewhere.

Whatever your vision of retirement is, you can be sure it includes one common denominator: freedom. Freedom from your job, from the demands of young children, from after school and weekend activities.

As you work towards your retirement goals, keep a couple of things in mind.

The first one is that what you consider a treat or a vacation now can quickly become a chore if that's all you ever get to do.

We know of a couple whose dream retirement was to spend lots of time at the lake house. They scrimped and saved all their lives to pay for their vacation home, and usually only spent a couple of weeks in the summer there.

When they retired, they sold their main home and moved into

their winterized lake house, only to discover that since it was a vacation spot, there was hardly ever anyone there during the week, and from Labor Day to Memorial Day, they were completely alone.

Add to that the fact that the roads weren't maintained in the winter and they had to drive over thirty miles for postal service and grocery shopping. They quickly discovered that what was a dream life during the summer was a nightmare at other times. Their idea of retirement was unrealistic.

Another person we know loves to travel. He and his first wife bought a time-share property and a motor home. However, when he remarried, this wife did not like to travel. She liked to stay near her family and the grandkids, especially on holidays and birthdays. His idea of traveling was quickly eroded into a few weeks here and there.

So how do you work out your retirement plans, especially if they differ from your spouse, since it is quite likely you weren't thinking about retirement when you remarried?

As with anything in marriage, it's best to talk about it before it becomes an issue. Then, look for creative ways to accommodate both perspectives of what constitutes the perfect retirement.

First consider your financial preparations. Are you setting yourselves up for failure by not planning at all? Social Security is not going to give you a retirement that will allow you to live in luxury. Another consideration is your home. You can figure out if you need to increase your payments now, while you are working, so that your home is paid off when you retire.

Other financial preparations include whether you will still be putting kids or grandkids through college on your retirement income. If so, you can start putting money into a college fund for them now.

Maybe you think you would like to sell the house and live in a motor home. Before you do that, rent or borrow one for a couple of weeks and give it a try. That way, you haven't burned your bridges if you find out it isn't the dream life you thought it was.

This kind of planning and experiencing beforehand applies to any radical change in living arrangements you are considering. Whether you want to spend the winters on the beach or in the mountains, try it for a week or so to see if you like it enough to live it all the time.

Maybe there is a hobby you think would be great to turn into a part-time job after you retire. Think about what makes it a hobby now. If it is a hobby because you like the freedom of setting it aside when you want to, remember that if it is a source of income after you retire, you may not be able to set it aside – you will have customers who are expecting a project when you promised it. If that changes your attitude towards the hobby, look for another source of income to depend on.

The most important thing is to seek God in what He would have you do. As an example, we have a friend who knows that God wants him to do missions work. As a result, he chose a job that provides him with free travel for life when he retires. He sees this as a way to be able to accomplish the missions work, and still have a useful career while he supports his family. During vacations, he and his wife have taken short-term missions trips to confirm God's calling on their lives. They are more committed than ever to being involved in missions when he chooses not to work at his job any longer.

Retirement might be as simple as changing careers. Our friend will go from being an aircraft mechanic to being a full-time missionary. He isn't retiring in the strictest sense of the word, because God still has work for him to do.

Retirement is not about sitting around waiting to die. Retirement is about being able to accomplish fully what God wants you to do without being tied down to a job. Retirement is about freedom to seek God's will in your life, and to follow it without reservation. This doesn't happen on the magic date you turn sixty-five – start planning for it now.

It is important that you not look forward to a particular date in the future and consider that as of that date, you no longer have any work to do. It is important to consider what God would have you do, what career changes He might make for you, and how you can bring about that transition as smoothly as possible. Your work for God is the most important job you have and the one with the best rewards

Lord, be my guide as I consider this next phase of my life. Speak clearly to me so that I know what You would have me do. Amen

Take-Away for Today

Sit down with your spouse and discuss all your ideas and dreams for your retirement. Plan as if money, health, and time were adequate to meet all your needs. Then, realistically look at what you are currently doing to make that a reality. Do not include potential winnings from lottery tickets, or possible inheritances, or any other form of income aside from what you are responsible for.

Look at how you can tailor your plans to meet your income and assets. For example, if one of your dreams is to travel, and you do not have the money to do that, consider a missions trip where the accommodations and food are paid for.

If you like to work with your hands, think about volunteering at a school that needs some shelving built. Like to read? Teach someone to read. If you like to work on cars, consider the local charity that accepts donated vehicles and then sells them. Like animals? Volunteer at an animal shelter. Like kids? Maybe a local church pre-school needs extra help. Are you an avid gardener? Check with your local civic gardens or community garden program.

His Joy, Her Joy, Our Joy

You will show me the path of life;
In Your presence is fullness of joy;
At Your right hand are pleasures forevermore.
(Psalm 16:11 NKJ)

Joy in the Journey

Go in peace. The LORD is pleased with your journey.
(Judges 18:6 NCV)

It is very easy to be joyful in a journey that starts on time, ends on time, and gets you where you want to go. Sometimes, though, the journeys of life are not so straightforward. There are diversions, sidetracks, detours, and circumstances that can threaten your carefully laid plans.

Recently, Donna had to travel by plane to a business meeting. When she got to the airport, she discovered that her plane had been delayed. The longer she sat waiting, the longer the delay got.

At first, passengers were told the plane was delayed by thirty minutes. Then, after waiting for an hour, they were told the plane was delayed due to inclement weather, and would be arriving in another hour. Half an hour after that announcement, it was revealed that the plane was still on the ground in Washington, DC, and would not arrive for another three hours.

Including the forty-five minute drive to the airport, the ninety minutes she waited for the scheduled departure time, the five hours waiting for the late flight, plus the ninety-minute flight time, she could have nearly driven to her destination in the same length of time.

The delay would have driven most people to distraction. In fact, at one point, several passengers left the waiting area to make arrangements on other airlines. Small children got fussy and fidgety, teens slept on the floor, and several business people made frantic phone calls to reschedule meetings and appointments.

Donna noticed that only one group of passengers seemed unfazed by the delay. A girls' soccer team, still hyped from a weekend tournament, found a way to put the delay to good use. They worked off their frustration by kicking a soccer ball back and forth.

They practiced inside and outside kicks, head bounces, and knee jamming saves. Occasionally their exuberance got the best of them, sending the ball screaming past reclining passengers.

Ignoring cautioning words from their coaches and the frowns of others nearby, these kids never lost their enthusiasm for the trip. While others struggled with keeping their peace, these teens found something profitable to do. They had an adventure, and the waiting passengers had a lesson in patience and peace.

Because if God is in control -- and He is -- then what do you need to be worried about? Sure, the plane got to its destination after 2 am, and everyone aboard lost a few hours' sleep, but Donna was still able to function cheerfully the next day and get the job done. She could have chosen to give in to the frustration of the situation, but instead she chose to have more journey to enjoy.

Your marriage can be just like this scheduled plane trip. You have a plan, you have your itinerary, and you have your destination. Then life happens. Many times, life events are beyond your control. Most people don't plan to have more than one marriage. And now here you are in your second, or maybe even your third or fourth marriage.

When life happens, as the old saying goes, you can see lemons or you can see lemonade. Choosing to make the best of each situation causes you to focus on what God is doing in the situation. A delayed plane trip might be something as simple as God protecting you from mechanical failure, or something as big as allowing you to minister to the single mother with three small children sitting next to you in the waiting area.

Many times, maybe you forget to ask God what His plan is. You have a job to do, a grocery list to complete, a lunch to host. What interest is God taking in the mundane things of your lives and your marriage? God takes a big interest in everything that concerns His kids. He knows that you make plans, and that sometimes those plans mesh with His.

So what can you do about enjoying this journey called marriage that God has placed you in? First, find out what plan God has for your marriage. You know He wants the marriage to succeed, to draw you closer to Him and to your spouse, to build a strong family relationship with your children.

But beyond that, just what does God care about your marriage? He cares very much, because marriage is not just about you. Marriage is also about the testimony you give the world about a loving God. Marriage is a demonstration of the relationship God wants to have with you. Marriage proves that not everyone has to be a cookie cutter duplicate of everyone else. After all, you seldom are duplicates of your spouse. In fact, God seems to take great delight in matching up the most unlikely man and woman and call them a couple.

Your marriage shows the world that opposites not only attract, but can stick it out. It shows the world that two are stronger together than separately. Your children will see just how loving and forgiving God is. Other see that a promise made can be kept, no matter how strong the temptation not to.

When you make a point of looking beyond the circumstances to the outcome, you will be able to see that the journey doesn't begin when you reach your destination. The journey begins with one small decision, to see God in everything you do, everywhere you go.

Make a point of looking for the silver lining in the cloud, for the rainbow in the storm, for the lemonade when all you seem to have are lemons. Choose to see the best in all situations, and enjoy the journey.

God, You are amazing that you would choose me to join You on this journey called marriage. Show me my marriage through Your eyes. Let me see You in all I do. Amen.

Take-Away for Today

It is easy to enjoy a vacation that is well-planned and researched down to the tiniest detail. It is easy to be caught up in the destination, and forget about the journey. If you are the type of person who likes to know the room number of every hotel you are going to sleep in while on vacation, then set aside the research and travel guides, and do the following:

Open the atlas, close your eyes, and place your finger on the page. Go there on your next vacation, with no preparation except travel arrangements. Figure out if you are going to drive or fly, when you are going, and then just go. Leave the details to God and enjoy the time.

If you are the type of person who believes that vacations are the time to throw away the rulebook, then do the opposite. Make a list of the things you want to do on a vacation, and then do some research about the best way to accomplish as many of those items on your list as you can within your vacation time. Pack as much into every day as you possibly can, knowing that the plan will probably change along the way.

The idea here is to do it differently than you are used to. There is no right or wrong way to take a vacation – the only wrong thing is a wrong attitude.

The Spice of Life

How much better are your expressions of love than
wine and the fragrance, of your perfume than any spice.
(Song of Solomon 4:10 God's Word)

Like many marriages, perhaps you try to divide the work
required to keep the household running smoothly. Regardless of how
the work is divided, though, there will always be times of
inconsistencies, where it seems that one party to the agreement is not
keeping up their end of the bargain. This can happen when you get
overwhelmed by the other things going on around you, including
physical, emotional, and even spiritual obstacles.

One of the ways we choose to divide the major task of meal
preparation is to decide who will cook which meal. This works well
for us because we both work in the home, and so are generally
together for each meal. It also works well for Patrick because he
likes a cooked breakfast, and well, for Donna, breakfast most days
could be just a cup of coffee. So, in the interest of his own well-
being, Patrick cooks breakfast.

We generally eat our larger meal at noon time, and since
Patrick makes breakfast, Donna makes what we call dinner. The
evening meal, what you call supper, is a catch-as-catch-can affair,
usually consisting of snacking, a piece of fruit, or something simple
like hot dogs or soup. If we are working away from home where we
cannot get home for dinner at noon, we eat our larger meal in the
evening. Even our best-laid plans are not written in concrete – we try
to be flexible.

Most of the time this plan works out really well. However,
recently, Donna stood in the middle of the kitchen at the end of the
day, staring at the range like it was the first time she'd ever seen it.
She was exhausted, having worked hard that day, and things had not
gone well. We had argued over something stupid, and Donna was

feeling overwhelmed and under-equipped to deal with anything else. She was even past the point of just plopping the chicken in a pan to bake. Or maybe it was just a tinge of guilt over the argument earlier that day.

The kind of tinge we're talking about is the kind where you feel justified in your feelings, but not in your actions. That little tug where you know you are right, and yet you know you did not handle it the way you should have. The tousling in your spirit where you want to make things right without admitting you were wrong.

Well, in this case, Donna knew that even though she thought she might have been right in her position, she was wrong in her reaction. And that really made her wrong in her position. Arguing with your spouse, even if they are dead wrong, is not how God treats you when you are wrong. Gently but firmly He speaks the truth, and then leaves you to ponder and meditate on that truth. It is always easier to come to the realization that you are wrong on your own.

Donna knew she was wrong, and so she wanted to make amends by having something special for supper. Still, she really did not have the energy to follow a recipe or the desire to remember an old favorite. In desperation, she turned to God, as she should have done much earlier in the day, and prayed, "God, please help. I'm overwhelmed, and I cannot think".

Instantly her mind cleared, and she began searching the refrigerator for ingredients. God directed her to take several different items that she would not normally put together, to baste the chicken with it, and bake it. Then He showed her a new way with potatoes that once again took ingredients she wouldn't have thought to combine, and create a new potato dish that you have come to enjoy often. The kitchen smelled wonderful, and Donna felt like Julia Childs in her prime – smart, successful, witty, invigorated.

The resulting meal was delicious. Patrick appreciated the extra time invested in the meal, and afterwards we discussed the day, the argument, and Donna's feelings of being overwhelmed. Patrick hadn't seen how Donna was feeling, but God had. And much better than a vacation, or any other artificial restorative, was God's plan. He knows who you are in Him, and you just needed to be reminded.

This experience showed us that God will take unlikely ingredients, combine them together, and make them work. After all, He took you as individuals, combined you under His guidance and love, and created a marriage that is a testimony to His grace and mercy.

The Bible tells you that your expressions of love are better than wine, more pleasing than spices. When you allow God to be the spice in your marriage, He can cook up a far better recipe for success and love than you ever could on your own. After all, His love is better than wine and more pleasing than spices, and He showers you with Himself as often as you will partake.

Loving God, thank You for loving me, blemishes and all. Thank You for cooking up bigger and better things in my life. Make me willing to receive from You. Amen.

Take-Away for Today

Make a date night with your spouse, and start with sharing the cooking for the evening, no matter whose turn it is to cook. Try this recipe, and see how these spices that you wouldn't normally combine together make the whole meal taste better.

Recipes:

Honey Ginger Chicken

½ c soy sauce
½ c honey
1 Tb ground ginger
2 lbs. chicken

Combine all in measuring cup. Pour over chicken pieces. Bake at 350 degrees for 50 minutes or until juices run clear. Serves 3-4

Ginger Garlic Potatoes

Cooking tip: to reduce the frying time for the potatoes, partially microwave them first.

3 baking/cooking potatoes, scrubbed, cut into 1 inch chunks
½ c olive oil
2 cloves chopped garlic or equivalent dry or bottles minced garlic
½ T ground ginger
variations: add ½ c chopped onion, ½ lb fresh sliced mushrooms, ½ c. chopped bell peppers with potatoes

Heat oil. Toss in remaining ingredients. Fry until golden and crispy. Serves 3-4

What's Missing Here?

Be happy with what you have because God has said,
"I will never abandon you or leave you."
(Hebrews 13:5 NAS)

As in most areas of life, it is easy to become discontented in your remarriage. This is particularly true if your expectations are colored by either your previous experience with marriage, or by your notion of what the perfect marriage should be like.

For most people, their first marriage was a time of discovery, a period when you were doing many things for the first time. From choosing your first china pattern to buying your first bedroom suite, choices were made based on your budget and style preferences.

Then you moved onto the big decisions of life, such as buying your first house and naming your first child. These choices affect you much longer than the color of your living room or the pattern of your wallpaper.

When it comes to your second marriage, however, most of these choices are not new to you. Second marriages can entail a completely new set of choices to be made, including where the kids go to college, whose house you live in, and where you invest for your retirement.

These decisions are, in some ways, more life-changing in a second marriage because they involve two people who have already had some experience in making big decisions, and will often have completely different outcomes in mind.

Regardless of why your first marriage ended, you bring a set of experiences into this second marriage that may be completely different than your spouse's. Where in your first marriage you were both likely inexperienced in many areas of married life such as finances, running a household, family life, and even sexual intimacy, in this marriage you both bring ideas of how things should be done.

This means that in your second marriage the things you let slide before can easily become a huge cause of disagreement now. You don't want to just settle for mediocre in any area of your life. It is not unusual to expect to duplicate the good parts of your previous marriage in your remarriage. In fact, it is easy to try to duplicate all the good memories while avoiding anything that led up to the bad.

While there is nothing wrong with wanting your second marriage to be equal to all the good of your first marriage, and better than any bad, you could well be setting yourselves up for failure.

Discontentment comes from comparing your situation to another situation that has different variables, including the people involved. You are not married to your first spouse, and any other marriage you might compare this one to does not involve the same people.

Other factors include age, health, finances, family structure, and even likes and dislikes. you cannot expect to duplicate the good memories of your first marriage, for example, by insisting that you vacation in the same places that you used to go to.

When you find yourselves asking, 'What is missing in my marriage?', the first thing to do is to thank God that those things that you did not like in your previous marriage are also absent.

If you are feeling discontented in any area, look at yourself first. It takes two to tango, and if you are not changing in some area then you are bound to repeat the same mistakes repeatedly.

Even if you believe that the problem is that you married someone just like your previous spouse, remember this: you married them. You chose them, you committed to them.

If discontentment is threatening to steal your happiness, the first thing to do is to stop comparing. It does not matter. The next thing to do is to look at what changes you are willing to make in yourselves. Discontent never begins with someone else – it always begins in you. As you consider the changes you believe need to be made, compare that with God's plan and direction for your life. If it does not agree with that, it is wrong.

A major source of discontent is unrealistic depictions of a perfect marriage. If you are comparing your marriage with something you saw on TV or read about in a novel, realize neither of these sources are good reality checks.

Discontentment is usually an overall feeling that something isn't right. You cannot put your finger on exactly what the problem is. Discontentment is a plan of the enemy to steal your happiness. Contentment is a frame of mind that says 'no matter what, I choose to do what is right'.

What is right is what God has in mind for you. If you believe that God has put this remarriage together, you will also believe He will do what is needed to keep it together. God is in the business of restoration and resurrection. Allow Him time and room in your marriage to restore what the enemy has stolen, and to resurrect your love for your spouse.

God, You are the prime example of a loving marriage relationship. As the bride of Christ, I know I am cherished by You. Show me how to demonstrate that love to my spouse. Amen.

Take-Away for Today

Independently of your spouse, write down the top three areas of your marriage where you experience the most discontentment. Beside each one, make a note of how you can change to correct that, how your spouse can change, and how you as a couple can change.

Pray about each of these items and changes, asking God to show you which area to deal with.

As a couple, compare your lists and changes, and discuss how to implement them, one at a time. Remember that this is to be a time of growth, not a time of tearing down. Even if your spouse is completely at fault, there must be some way for you to change as well.

Time for You

Step out of the traffic! Take a long, loving look
at me, your High God.
(Psalm 46:10 The Message)

When you first marry, it is an exciting time of discovery. You learn more about your spouse and about yourselves as you adjust your lifestyles to fit each other. Sometimes these adjustments are lifestyle changes, and sometimes they involve actually trying to fit two households into one, or turn two separate families into one cohesive unit.

Marriage is the joining of two individuals into one, in a spiritual sense. You understand that you do not morph into some new body with two heads and four arms. Rather, the union is spiritual and emotional. This is God's perfect plan for marriage.

Unfortunately, you do not always follow that plan completely. Sometimes you take the concept of marriage, and try to make it fit into your idea of what marriage should be. We have all seen marriages where you wonder why they got married in the first place. Each one still maintains their own bank accounts, goes on separate vacations, has his and her cars, his and her families, his and her churches. One thing that you have seen in this type of marriage is that there never seems to be enough to go around – not enough money, time, or energy. Somehow in the dividing of the assets of the marriage, something is lost.

Then there are those couples where one completely dominates the other, to the extent that there seems to be only one person in the marriage. The other cannot think for themselves, cannot do anything without the other's permission.

Neither of these examples is God's choice. First and foremost, He created you to have a relationship with him. He chose you from the beginning of time, and He filled you with His spirit.

Sometimes what happens is that you think that you are filled with God's spirit, and that is enough to maintain your marriage. And so you depend entirely on your spouse now to keep you filled. However, just like a water jug, in order to be able to stay full, either you need to not give anything out, or you need to be refilled from a larger reservoir from time to time.

If you choose not to give anything out and are not refilled with a new anointing from God, you will grow stagnant and moldy, just like an old rain barrel that has not had fresh water poured into it. This happens when you neglect your private, couple, and family time with God, when you choose not to be involved in a church or fellowship, and when you believe that you can do it on your own.

Unless you are refilled from time to time, eventually you are going to be spiritually empty. And when you are empty of the Spirit of God, you won't be able to give anything good to others. The Spirit of God does not just give you scripture verses to quote. A true filling by the Holy Spirit prepares you physically, spiritually, and emotionally for the demands placed on you as a spouse, parent, friend, employee – in all areas of your lives. The Holy Spirit enables you to accomplish much more than you could have been able to do by yourselves.

Spending time alone with God, apart from your spouse, gives you the time to get your spiritual and emotional reserves filled. When you are full of God, you are able to support and bolster your spouse. Just as God pours Himself out on you, His plan is for you to give to others and to receive from time to time.

Spending quiet time with God may seem like a selfish thing to do, given your busy schedules and hectic lifestyles. However, it is the best thing you can do for your marriage.

Lord, forgive me for neglecting my time with You. Thank You for showing me that I can be a better spouse when I am filled with Your spirit. Amen.

Take-Away for Today

Buy a devotional book that you know will interest your spouse, one they can do on their own, and give it as a "just because" gift. There are many to choose from, such as for golfers, fishermen, grandparents, teachers, moms, dads, and so on. Then choose one for yourself that will interest you. Go to separate rooms, or choose a separate time of day to spend time with God, using the devotional book as a springboard to where God would lead you.

This quiet time for yourself is not meant to replace your prayer time as a couple or as a family. It is meant to replenish your spirit for what you have already given out.

Then, when you come back together as a couple, share what you have learned in your own private quiet time, and seek ways to apply it in your marriage.

His Battle, Her Battle, Our Victory

Let marriage be held in honor among all.
(Hebrews 13:4 ASV)

Waiting for the Bus

Take up the whole armor of God, that you may be able to withstand in the evil day, and having done all, to stand.
(Ephesians 6:13 NKJ)

For those who drive on a regular basis, waiting for the bus can seem like cruel and unusual punishment. In many cases, you have to stand out in the open, no matter what the weather. It seems like the bus stop you are standing at might well be the only one in the city that does not have a shelter.

Then there are the people who are sharing the bus stop with you. Auto-drivers develop a sense of snobbishness, and regular bus riders can sense that. They know that you are not a regular, and that you are in foreign territory.

And what about those schedules and routes? Why is it they never get you where you want to go when you want to be there? You either get to your destination so early that you need to rent a hotel room, or else you are racing through the lobby on the way to a really important meeting. And it never seems you can get where we're going on just one bus.

Marriage is a lot like a bus ride, especially for the remarried. You are not complete novices at marriage, so, like someone who rides the bus once every two or three years, you have an idea of how to behave at the bus stop and how to put your money into the fare box.

We understand the concept of marriage, of some of the inner workings of two people sharing the same living space, and even of the cost to make the marriage a success.

However, as remarrieds, you can sometimes bring a romantic notion into your marriage of how it should be. Just like the occasional bus rider who can see that new upholstery on the seats would make this experience a whole lot more interesting, you can think that there are lots of areas of improvement you will implement this time around.

After all, you have some experience at marriage, at the successes and the failures of the process, and surely you can improve on it to make this time around better than the last.

But just like trying to tell your bus driver that he should take a shortcut you know about so that you won't be late for work, marriage isn't all about you and your convenience.

First, you did not design marriage, God did. As the master designer, He has the right to make changes to the plan, you do not. And just like a bus route, which someone designed with the benefit of many in mind, marriage is meant to benefit many.

Marriage is not the fulfillment of your every whim and desire. It cannot be, unless your every whim and desire is in complete accord with God. And few can lay claim to that.

And just like a bus ride, where you have to learn to get along with the other riders on your bus, marriage requires you to accommodate your life with your spouse and your children and new in-laws and all the rest of the people who come with that.

If you do not learn to get along with them, your ride will be most uncomfortable, for you and for them. In marriage, your plans must include the benefit of others, just like a bus route. Getting the most people to their ultimate destination, in this case, a relationship with God, is the goal of marriage. God designed marriage to show the world what a relationship with Him looks like. Showing people a loving God who wants to know you intimately is something the world needs to know about.

Marriage requires you to be prepared to follow God's plan, to be willing to include others in that plan, to acknowledge there is a price to pay to be married, and to realize that no matter how good they may look, your plans are not necessarily God's plans.

Sometimes your marriage feels like you are standing at a bus stop in the middle of a snowstorm. All around you, the rest of the world has disappeared, and all you can see is the storm. It is as if it will never end. When that is your marriage, choose to withstand this assault. Sure, you could take the easy way out and call a cab, but that too has a cost. Looking for the easy way out of a situation in your marriage is often more costly than sticking it out. Every marriage goes through some storms. When that happens, bow your head against the snow, and pray.

Sometimes it might seem as if the people around you are the problem. After all, if it were not for them, life would be so much easier. Of course, they might be saying the same thing, that if it was not for you, their lives would be so much easier. Instead of trying to fit everyone into your idea of what they should be, focus on yourself and how you might need to change.

This doesn't mean you are to compromise on moral issues. This is about dissatisfaction with the people in your life, who don't quite meet your expectations. Cut them some slack – you probably aren't what they would have chosen, either.

There can be times when it seems your marriage is on the rails. Just like when you are riding the bus because your car is in the shop. You hope it is only going to be a day or so, and then it becomes a week, and then you cannot afford to pay the bill, and you have to keep riding the bus. In the same way, your marriage can hit a temporary diversion where you keep hoping things are going to get better, but you cannot see it yet.

Who says you have to see it? Did God put this marriage together or not? If you believe He did, then God says that whatever is meant for bad, He will turn to good. That means that whatever you are going through right now will make you a better spouse and will make your marriage stronger.

Just like a bus ride, marriage costs time and money, it costs compromise and energy. But just like meeting an old friend at the stop who you had lost touch with, marriage draws you closer to God, to rely on Him like never before in your life, and to reach out and touch lives that wouldn't have been possible without the marriage.

So when marriage feels like the bus ride from hell, remember that God is in the driver's seat, and He has everything under control. Sit back and enjoy the ride – He'll take you places you never thought possible.

God, forgive me for trying to be in control of this marriage. Show me how to relax in Your hands, and to enjoy the scenery along the way. Amen.

Take-Away for Today

As a couple, plan out a day trip on the local bus system. If you don't have a local system, choose a day trip on the Greyhound Bus or its equivalent. No bus? Try the train instead. You do not have to go far, just go. Plan what you want to do when you get there, pack a picnic lunch if you choose, and determine you will have a fun time. Take in a ball game or go bowling, see a movie, or just walk around the lake. If you have kids or grandkids, take them along, too.

As you go, make notes of what you see, smell, hear, feel, and think. Take pictures. Treat this day as if you were a tourist, discovering a new part of your city or region.

At the end of the day, compare your notes. Talk about the ways you each experienced the day that was different, such as a smell you missed, or a thought you had about people you saw. These different perceptions will help you understand more about yourself, your spouse, your family, and your relationship. Then discuss those things that you all made note of. This will confirm that you are alike in several different areas.

United you Stand

No weapon formed against you shall prosper,
And every tongue which rises against you in judgment
You shall condemn.
(Isaiah 54:17 NKJ)

Our neighbor has several large trees on their property that attract squirrels. We like to watch the squirrels as they perform their aerial acrobatics in the trees. However, we do not want them on our property. These squirrels clamber all over our neighbor's house, and every time we see one heading for our shared fence, we scare them off.

Don't get us wrong – we like squirrels when they are being what squirrels are supposed to be – tree-dwelling rodents. What we do not like is when they try to infiltrate our living quarters by nesting in our attic and making a nuisance of themselves.

That's when we forget about the tree-dwelling part, and remember they are rodents, not very different, in our minds, to mice and rats. Squirrels are an example of those things that are good when they are doing what they are supposed to do, and nuisances when they aren't.

There might well be tree-dwelling squirrels and attic-dwelling squirrels in your marriage. Tree-dwelling squirrels are those things that are in order, are in moderation, and are doing what they are supposed to do. One example is fellowship time with people in your church. When you spend time ministering and being ministered to, it can be very easy for this tree-dwelling squirrel to become an attic-dwelling version.

Neglecting your family and your spouse in favor of spending time with folks from church shows that things have gotten out of order.

We have often tried to peek through our shared fence at the neighbor's yard to see why they have so many squirrels. We do not know if they have a bird feeder out, or if they leave garbage lying around. Maybe it is something as simple as the kids leaving food outside or the fact they don't have a cat or a dog. Any or all of these factors could well contribute to the squirrel population on the other side of our boundary.

Leaving garbage around is a picture of allowing trash to clutter your life, such that it attracts pests. This could include bad habits, ungodly friends, or just your desire to keep up with the Joneses.

Something as simple and innocent as having a bird feeder could attract unwanted pests. In your marriage, this might be the way you dress, for example. You tell yourself you dress a certain way for your spouse, when really it is attracting undesirable attention from others.

Kids can be the reason why unwanted pests show up at your door. Know who your children are friends with, and know their parents. Monitor those friendships, and, if needed, restrict who your kids choose to hang around with. As parents, you are responsible for setting the ground rules, and children want boundaries.

When you take authority over your home and family, you will meet resistance. Most people enjoy squirrels; some even purposely feed them to encourage them to hang around.

As for us , we wish we had a small BB gun to pop them off the fence when they get too close. That is the way to treat any pests that come into your lives, your marriage, or your home. God has created you with a warrior spirit to fight anything that does not look like Him. Take control today, and watch God fight your biggest battles for you.

Remember, there is no such thing as a cute attic-dwelling squirrel.

Almighty God, fill me with Your warrior spirit, to defend my home, my marriage, and my family against the attack of the enemy. Amen

Take-Away for Today

Consider what attic-dwelling squirrels may have been allowed to sneak into your marriage. Especially consider the ones that do not seem to be out of control right now. Anything that you preface with 'I could give it up' or 'I can control it' has the potential to take over your life.

Fast from some major part of your relaxation for the next thirty days. This could be TV, reading, sports, excessive sleeping – whatever you consider is your primary source of relaxation or reward for working hard. Replace it with family time, hobbies, or projects around your home that you can do together as a couple or as a family.

The Highways and the Byways

True to Your word, You let me catch my breath,
and send me in the right direction.
(Psalm 23:3 The Message)

Living in, or having visited, a large city, you know about the roadways that intersect the cities. As cities spread out, you still want to get to where you are going in the same amount of time it took you to get there five or ten years ago.

Traffic reports start before the sun rises, and often don't end until well into the evening. And every day sounds much like the day before. An accident westbound on this highway, a stalled vehicle on that interstate, a rollover on this road, and an accident with injuries at another main intersection. Only the locations seem to vary slightly.

It sounds like driving to work is a very dangerous proposition. Traveling anywhere in the city has come to be more dangerous than an African safari.

And if you listen to the media about marriage, it sounds like marriage is an even more dangerous adventure. From infidelity to divorce, from death to financial destruction, marriage sounds like it is destined to fail.

And without God, it is. Without the leading and direction of the Holy Spirit, every route will lead in failure. Without the love of Christ to give and receive, you are assured of major problems.

We do not get in your car to go to work expecting to have an accident on the way. But one moment of indecision, one lapse of attention, and you can find yourselves going over the edge. In the same way, no one gets remarried expecting to have this marriage end in divorce or the death of your spouse. Being attentive to your marriage will keep it intact.

Keeping your attention on God will keep your focus where it needs to be – on your relationships. Desiring to please Him will result in doing what's best for your spouse. This doesn't mean doing whatever your spouse wants. Just as cutting across lanes of traffic to get to the off ramp you need will cause havoc on the roads, selfishness in your marriage will undo your best efforts.

Selfishness is the major cause of the end of marriages. When you feel you are not getting what you deserve out of the relationship, you will seek other ways to satisfy. A prime indicator of selfishness is infidelity. Infidelity is not always manifested as adultery. You can seek gratification and edification from someone other than your spouse in other ways, including time spent, your thoughts, and your conversations. Any time you look outside your marriage relationship, which includes God and your spouse, to bolster your self-worth, you are wrong. If you look at your marriage as the representation on earth of your relationship with God, ask yourselves how you want God to treat you. Do you want Him to drop you like a hot potato if He isn't satisfied with how you treat Him? If not, you can see that looking anywhere else than your marriage is wrong.

The second leading cause of divorce is financial pressures. When you owe a lot of money, or you spend too much money, you get caught in a bind that forces you to work more to pay the bills. God never designed you to be in slavery to things – you are called to be servants to Christ, not to credit.

If you spend too much money, or if you have too many bills and not enough money, getting another job or working more hours is not going to help. Cut the spending. Financial destruction is not an accident: it is the result of not planning.

If you heard about an accident on the road that you normally take to get to work, you would look for other ways to get to work that avoid that accident. You know that getting in the line of traffic behind the accident will not get you to work. In the same way, once you recognize that you are about to crash into financial ruin, decide not to keep going the way you are going, hoping it clears up by the time you get there.

Instead, take positive action. Trade in your cars for vehicles that will have lower payments, lower insurance, and lower fuel costs. Stop buying stuff on credit. Limit your eating out, set a grocery budget, and eat some of the stuff in your freezer or pantry.

Just like your trip to get to work every day, there are many ways to avoid adding to the stresses on your marriage. God's desire is for success in your marriage, and the enemy's desire is for the marriage to fail. When it feels like you are under attack, recognize that you are. Choose to do something about it.

Start with checking your relationship with God. Get more serious about seeking His direction for all areas of your life. Spend time with your spouse in prayer and devotions. Talk about your situation, and make plans for you both to participate in the solution. When you start with God, including Him in all of these plans, and follow His leading, you will be able to watch the enemy flee.

God, there are areas of my marriage I have neglected because it makes me uncomfortable. Please reveal those to me, and show me Your plan for victory. Amen.

Take-Away for Today
Because infidelity and finances are such an attack on marriage, it is critical to deal with it before it becomes an issue.

As a couple, make the commitment to stand firm against any hint of infidelity in any area of your lives. Infidelity does not have to mean adultery. It can be as seemingly innocent as confiding in a friend things you have not told your spouse, or choosing to spend time with friends instead of your spouse.

Commit to a date night with your spouse once a week, where you can share things you like to do together. This doesn't have to be something that costs money. A walk in the park, watching a movie at home, or dancing together in the dark are all great ways to spend time together without costing you any money.

However, the investment of time and emotion will pay off handsomely.

Join the Celebration

I will shout for joy and sing your praises, for you have redeemed me.
(Psalm 71:23 NLT)

We have all seen sports games where someone in the crowd seems to get carried away in their support of their favorite team. On a recent football game, fans painted their faces and chests in their team colors and wore big foam hats and fingers. One of the fans tried to run across the football field. His enthusiasm was rewarded by being led away in handcuffs.

And this enthusiasm is not limited to major league games. Recently in the news there was a story about a little league mother who shot and killed another mother over an argument about whose son had caused the other team to score.

Even in the church, you can see examples of getting carried away with praising things that are temporary. At a recent Super Bowl party, Donna, who likes to tease the people who are really getting into the game, made the comment, "It's only a game. It's not going to change any of your lives." Her comment was met with dropped jaws and wide-eyed stares.

As a remarried couple and family, you have many opportunities in your lives to praise many people and things that are not going to change your lives. Your focus must be on praising those who really do make a difference.

First, you must praise God. He alone is worthy of your praise. Without God, you would not be able to operate in the peace and assurance of your salvation, of your forgiveness, and of your being changed into something better.

Praise to God is not limited to your time in church. Consider your entire lives to be a song of praise to your King. Strive to always honor and glorify Him in all you do, all you say, and all you think. The world is looking to you for an example, and you must be sure to provide them with one that is on a strong Biblical foundation.

It is easy to praise when you are feeling good about God, your marriage, your family, and yourselves. However, the Bible tells you to bring a sacrifice of praise. When you don't feel good about God or anything else, you are to praise Him anyway. No matter how you feel, you can still find something to praise God for, even if it is something as trivial as the sunrise this morning, or the moon at night.

It is also easy to praise your spouse when they are doing a good job, when they are being attentive to your needs and desires, and when they treat you right. It is easy to praise them for working hard, or for doing the chores.

It is harder to praise them when you do not see a good outcome to their actions. When you do not want to praise your spouse, that is the very time when it is necessary to search until you find something praiseworthy, no matter how small. Even if it is something like thanking them for putting the top back on the toothpaste this morning, that is a beginning.

We once read about a woman whose husband snored up a storm at night as he slept. For nearly forty years, she lay awake for many hours at night as he sawed the logs, oblivious to her discomfort. She spent much of that lost sleep time praying that God would stop the snoring. Then her husband died, and she found she could not sleep at night without his snoring to lull her to sleep.

This woman should have been thanking God for a husband. She should have been praying that God would close her ears so she could fall asleep. Maybe she could have been looking for solutions, such as going to bed first, so she would be asleep before he started snoring.

There will always be reasons to find fault in what your spouse, your children, and even in what God is doing in your life. Rather than looking for ways to complain, look for ways to praise each one, and to lift them up instead of tear them down. Set the example for them of how you want to be treated, and set the example to the world of how God should be treated.

Forgiving Father, thank You for showing me that You deserve my praise whether I feel like it or not. Show me ways to praise You, my spouse, and my children. Amen.

Take-Away for Today

Independently, make a list of the top ten things you love about your spouse, and the top ten things you would like to see changed in them. Tonight, before you go to bed, thank them for those ten things you like. Then, each night before you go to sleep, thank them for another ten things that you remembered. Pray for them privately for the ten things you would like to see changed. Let God be the solution, and let Him show you areas where you might need to change.

As a couple, make a list of the top ten things you love about each of your children, and tell them about this list during family devotional time or over dinner. As a couple, make a list of the top ten things you would like to see changed, and pray about this list each day together as a couple.

Watch and see how quickly the praise brings about more things to love them for, and how quickly God will answer your prayers for change. Remember, too, that your spouse has made a similar list for you, so expect to hear some good things, and to see some changes in yourself.

www.ingramcontent.com/pod-product-compliance
Lightning Source LLC
Chambersburg PA
CBHW071859020426
42331CB00010B/2593